Lisa Appignanesi was born in Poland and grew up in France and Canada. A novelist and writer, she is Chair of the Freud Museum, London, Visiting Professor of Literature and the Medical Humanities at King's College London, and former President of English PEN. Her non-fiction includes *All About Love: Anatomy of an Unruly Emotion*; the prize-winning *Mad, Bad and Sad: A History of Women and the Mind Doctors from 1800 to the Present*; and *Freud's Women* (with John Forrester). She is one of the editors of *Fifty Shades of Feminism*. Her most recent novel is the fin-de-siècle *Paris Requiem*. *Trials of Passion*, a book on the intersection of madness, the law and psychiatry in crimes of passion, will be published in 2014. Lisa Appignanesi was awarded an OBE for services to literature in January 2013.

LOSING THE DEAD

Lisa Appignanesi

virago

This edition pu

First published in Grea

Copyright ©

The moral right

A CIP catalogue record for this book
is available from the British Library.

ISBN 978-1-84408-929-1

Typeset in Garamond by M Rules
Printed and bound in Great Britain by
Clays Ltd, St Ives plc

Papers used by Virago are from well-managed forests
and other responsible sources.

MIX
Paper from
responsible sources
FSC® C104740
www.fsc.org

Virago Press
An imprint of
Little, Brown Book Group
100 Victoria Embankment
London EC4Y ODY

An Hachette UK Company
www.hachette.co.uk

www.virago.co.uk

For my parents
Hena and Aron,
and their grandchildren,
Abigail and David
Josh and Katrina

Is it possible that the antonym of 'forgetting' is not 'remembering,' but *justice*?

Yosef Hayim Yerushalmi

CONTENTS

Legacies

Legacies

In my father's last days, he transformed the ordinary London
hospital ward where he lay into an SS camp. The white-
coated doctors became black-uniformed officers, their boots
hammering over floorboards with deadly intent as they
approached his cell. Medical implements were instruments of
torture, the oxygen mask a purveyor of poison gas. My
momentarily absent mother was a whore servicing the ranks –
whether willingly or not was a moot point. In any case, she was
not altogether to be trusted. Only I was and I would help him
to get out of here.

His hand gripped my wrist. His eyes, two glistening points
of feverish pleading in an ashen face, gazed at me in desperation. He seemed to know me, though I didn't know who that
me was meant to be, a sister not yet lost, perhaps. He spoke in
Yiddish – a language he hadn't used to address me in for over
thirty years. And he spoke with a flat, grim certainty, his voice
a hoarse whisper emerging from some depth of pain and history. Occasionally, he would raise his head from the pillow and
with a tense alertness echoed in the bite of his fingers, would

check to see whether one of 'them' was listening. My rational protests were shushed into stillness.

A day earlier he had tried to make his escape, a pyjama-clad figure breaking out from the confines of University College Hospital into the freedom of the streets. He had been brought back – by an informer in cahoots with my mother. But that night, with my help, his escape would be certain.

It was that night he died. November 20, 1981.

The content of my father's diabetic delirium shook me. He hadn't talked of the war years since my childhood. Yet at the end, they were there intact – like some wilfully obscured and venomous secret, which all his later experience couldn't obliterate. A slight shift of the kaleidoscope of consciousness and those distant years surfaced, still charged with enough raw emotion to propel his hallucinatory fantasies. Terror, for him, always came in uniform.

A year after his death we made what was in fact a ritual visit to my father's grave. For Jews, the passage of a year marks the time when the tombstone is consecrated and though, as a family, we had almost no religion, my father had more than the rest. He is buried in the Northern Synagogue Cemetery, a flat expanse of land off Bullsmoor Lane on the outskirts of London. As we walked and walked through the cemetery's bare, windswept symmetry of ranked stone and pebbled paths unrelieved by tree or flower, my son, who was then seven, talked about his grandfather. He remembered that his grandpa in his last years had repeatedly complained, particularly as he struggled up the steep incline of

Highgate West Hill, that his feet were killing him. I explained that his grandfather suffered from an illness called diabetes which often hinders the circulation of blood to the extremities. Josh shot a mischievous glance in my direction. Already adept at what was to become his characteristic spiky humour, he wickedly suggested that we should inscribe his grandfather's tombstone with the epitaph, 'His feet killed him.'

We all giggled, relieved at the sound in that dank, silent place. Yet as I gazed at that tombstone with its etched inscription of 'Born in Poland, 4 October 1913 – died, London, 20 November 1981', it came to me that my son's joke had more than a degree of truth in it. In a way my father's feet had killed him. War had chased him from a small town on the outskirts of Warsaw, had hunted him from site to site through the considerable expanse of Poland. Its aftermath had transported him to France and then to Canada. And now, he lay buried in London, a city where he was an occasional visitor, and in a cemetery devoid of kin. He had always been a man in a hurry. Yet in all those years he had never been able to run quite fast enough to evade the grip of the past.

Almost two decades have passed since that final meeting with my father. I can still occasionally hear his hospital voice evoking a scene I could neither see nor altogether share. Its aura haunts me more persistently than it ought, perhaps because I can smell in it the shadowy, uncertain ground on which my mundane, largely Canadian and largely happy childhood was played out. I have never been particularly interested in that childhood. It seemed to me a dull place, full of arid stretches of empty time. I escaped from it as soon as I could, fled the embarrassing clutches of the family circle. Life was about pulling your socks up and facing the new, constructing a good enough existence as best as one could.

I still feel that. Yet as my son grows into adulthood and my daughter into adolescence, I find myself wanting to root in those early shadows – many of which bear the shape of my parents' experience. Partly because I want to be able to answer my children's questions about their family. Partly because I am confronted by the sense that mine is the last generation for whom the war is still a living tissue of memory rather than a dusty and barbaric history of facts and statistics. For my generation, born in the decade after 1945, the war will always be the Second World War.

Memory is an emotional climate, a thick set of sights and smells and sounds and imprinted attitudes which can pollute as well as clarify. In several parts of the world today, battles of ideas are being fought over how we remember the Second World War. Sometimes the ideas take up arms. In France, people still agonise over degrees of collaboration and complicity, what the immediate post-war years chose to bury along with the dead. The Poles have a festering need to be exonerated from some of their guilt in the Holocaust: they too, after all, were victims of the Nazis. In Israel, the Holocaust has become a holy litany: can its embattled survivors ever do any wrong? In the former Yugoslavia, old remembered enmities between partisans and Cetniks fuelled the ethnic strife. In Germany, many wonder whether bigger and better memorials to guilt are a simple way of shedding it, while neo-Nazi parties once again agitate for a homogeneous German population. In the United States, those concrete blocks of memory we call museums package the experience of the Holocaust so that everyone becomes a survivor. A paroxysm of wound-envy has led each group to seek out its own moment of irreparable damage: the Nanking Massacre for Chinese Americans, slavery for Afro-Americans. Unity, it seems, resides in suffering or its memory. And the word 'survivor' has entered common language, like 'trauma' – used to describe a multitude of forms of recovered everyday unhappiness which can be alleviated by healing therapies or support groups.

In its own small way, my family story touches on this whole complex tangle of remembering and forgetting. What measure is due to each in that tricky dance of time which is the making of a life?

It can hardly be coincidental that I want to remember, to uncover, to know, at the moment when my last gateway to family memory – my mother – is losing hers. Her bewilderment, as I try to press her on facts and dates which are always just out of her reach, is painful. She can only return and return again to what she has already told me, scraps of unruly experience which refuse the consecutive shape of story. Her memory has taken on the randomness of dream, unconstrained by any order or external prodding. Keeping pace with the increasing limitations of her daily life, it has also grown poorer in detail, so that I have to fill in from previous tellings the gaps in hers. Many still remain and have to be leapt over like holes in a worn pavement.

Sometimes her body remembers more than her mind: she will look up at me from eyes that are still deeply blue and strike a coquettish pose as if she were addressing some ghostly admirer whose name and face and place have long since vanished. I can read more from these startling gestures than from her words. She talks often to her father and to mine, she tells me, as if one could phone the dead on a daily basis, but too often they speak to her only of the weather. Perhaps in her dotage – that nice word which takes a cup of tea to senility and wraps a scarf round the cold throat of Alzheimer's – she has finally become English. It is to anchor myself against the rudderless ship of her mind, that I finally decide to write all this down. Writing has to entail some kind of order, even if the voyage into the past is always coloured by invention. Memory is also a form of negotiation.

There is more. In an act of reparation – since I am a bad daughter who refuses her mother both her present and much of her presence – I would like to give my mother's past back to her, intact, clear, with all its births and deaths and missing persons in place. The task, I know is impossible. The dead are lost. But maybe, none the less, it makes a difference if by remembering them, we lose them properly.

So this is a journey into my parents' past – into that foreign country they carried within themselves, which was also the country of war. The psychological tropes, the ways of confronting and filtering experience, which structured their lives grew largely out of that war and subsequent immigration. I suspect they passed these patterns on to my brother and me, as surely as they passed on their genes and with as little choosing. Understanding this transgenerational haunting is part of the journey – and perhaps in a century where migration, forced or chosen, is the norm, it is its most common part. Memory, like history, is uncontrollable. It manifests itself in unruly ways. It cascades through the generations in a series of misplaced fears, mysterious wounds, odd habits. The child inhabits the texture of these fears and habits, without knowing they are memory.

The journey is not a pleasure cruise, with its stopping points already marked out in good, linear fashion. In a sense it is more like an archaeological excavation. The objects sought for, alluded to in story, even documented in the formality of 'survivor interviews' or archives, may or may not be there, or they may be so written over by tales and memory and the passage of history, that one can only guess from the traces at their original use and shape.

Then, too, my mother's confusion is contagious. When she asks me, 'Do you remember your father?' as if I were a stranger who had never shared his life, I question my own shards of memory. But this is the only place I can begin.

PART ONE

Scenes of Memory

Arrival

M y family arrived in the port of Halifax, Nova Scotia on April 27, 1951. That much is certain. The red stamp of the Canadian Immigration authorities on the single remaining card provides a testimonial, though whether the 'third class' printed at the top of the yellowing rectangle refers to the class of landed immigrant we were or to our station on ship is unclear.

Official papers and government stamps play a significant part in this story. From the evidence of this card, their status as witnesses may be as unreliable as so much else. My brother's name appears in blue pencil. It must be my brother, since the 'Master' is clear and he was then twelve years old, too young for a Mr. But the name which follows has been written over, fudged by some official, perhaps perplexed by the slippage between Borensztejn, the Polish original of the family name and its later, more Germanic elision into Borenstein. The result on the card is neither one nor the other.

Identities, in my family, seem always to have been there for the making.

No one remembers the name of the ship which carried us. It probably sailed from Le Havre since we had spent nearly two years in Paris, waiting for the necessary immigration documents. To my five-year-old self, it was a vast pleasure dome, miraculously afloat on the blue heave and toss of the ocean. While my mother and brother, their faces pale from sea-sickness, lay huddled on deck chairs, my father and I cavorted, walked the length and breadth of seemingly eternal decks, played quoits and shuffleboard in sunlight. Perhaps the image of that distant passage is still vivid in my mind because my father was so distinctly happy. He must have felt released, free at last of what he used later to call 'the cemetery' that was all of Poland and a good part of Europe. Free, too, for the moment, of the anxieties of setting up life in yet another alien country, a process which would soon trigger more indignities and rage.

In his aura, I too was happy. I don't know whether I hadn't been earlier.

In Paris, while they did battle with immigrant life, my parents had sent me off to live with a farming family on the outskirts of Chantilly. There, apparently, I learned how to eat properly at mealtimes and how to speak French properly – both achievements being on a par. I had a duck to play with and various farmyard animals. A stern, large-boned Frenchwoman, with hair pulled back into a bun, looked after me and everything else. Meanwhile my brother, Stanley – though at that time he was Simon and had already been Stanislaw and Szolam – became a boarder at Maison Lafitte, a school for refugees run along socialist lines. Here, according to him, he perfected his playground fighting techniques and learned how to contend with a psychologist. The psychologist was English and thought my disobedient and uncooperative brother retarded, if not altogether mad. My brother perceived both him and the teachers as hostile. There seems to have been little insight into a boy's experience of displacement and war, let alone the additional turmoil caused by separation from his parents in a strange land and language. Stanley coped by escaping under the school fence and away to the village or by hiding in a grassy nook and reading. Pictures of him at the time show a staunch little dark-haired boy with a boxer's stance. In one he fingers a sling-shot. His chin is always determinedly thrust forward.

French in place, we both came back to Paris, where I was sent to a convent school. It was some fifteen minutes' short-legged stroll from our two-roomed apartment on the Rue des Archives. All I can recall of it is the dark-blue smock I wore, the too-tall stool on which I sat in order to read out stories to the other girls, busy with their sewing and embroidery. The sweet-faced, wimpled nuns had determined that I was good at reading and hopeless at sewing. Perhaps they had unwittingly determined my life.

Whether it was because I felt released from the confines of the convent school or simply because we were at last all together, the Atlantic, its odd salt-spray on my lips, felt good.

Our destination was Montréal, chosen for its Frenchness, though few of the Montréalers we met in those first months spoke French. My parents had failed to realise that in the parochial language politics of Québec, French was then not a language for Jews.

Quite why they had chosen to come to Canada remains something of a mystery. Canada necessitated a longer wait for papers than the United States where my father also had the possible boon of relatives. Yet Canada was the choice. It was my mother's apparently. In her narrative, she is always the decision-taker and her decisions are always taken on instinct and always right. And she chose Canada, it seems, because it was *terra incognita*, a blank whiteness, unmapped by myths, unpeopled by named individuals – a country whose reputation in Poland was simply one of comfort and plenty. I don't think either of my parents knew then that Canada was the name the Nazis had given to the commercial hub of the camp at Birkenau where the possessions of over a million dead – the trunks and string-wrapped parcels and blankets and pots and pans and valuables – were sifted and classified. They wouldn't have liked the irony. As the years went by, they were increasingly proud to be Canadian. My father, whose long-term Zionism had tugged him towards but never landed him in Israel, would even joke that when Moses, that lifelong stammerer, had designated the promised land as 'C ... C ... Canaan', it was only because he couldn't bring out all the syllables of 'Canada'.

At the central train station in Montréal, a lawyer awaited us. He had been sent by my father's brother in New York, who had also helped to arrange our papers. Some seventeen years older than my father, his brother, Abraham, had left Poland just after the First World War. Maybe the fact that my uncle hadn't made the journey himself, wasn't there to greet this small band of bewildered refugees, was one of the reasons for their increasingly sour relations. When they finally met again, after we had been in Canada for some months, his American brother treated my father a little too much like the member of the 'huddled masses' he undoubtedly was. And my father's pride rebelled. For years he would mutter that he had paid his brother over the top for his help. In retrospect, I imagine there was something both deeper and more usual in their hostilities. For those Jews who had quit Europe before the years of Nazi terror, their Eastern European kin brought with them to the new and shining world something of the taint and pollution and perfidy of persecution, an acrid whiff of the death camps. Guilt, mingled with not a little fear of contamination, surfaced with their proximity. It was almost as if it were better if they could be mourned or at least kept at arm's length by distant acts of charity. So the recent immigrants or refugees clung together – of necessity. I cannot remember a single friend of my parents in those early years in Montréal who was already a Canadian – a person who didn't speak with an accent.

By the summer of '51, we were ensconced on Esplanade, a street of three-storey terraced brick and stone houses, with the steep outdoor staircases typical of nineteenth-century Québec architecture. It was then an immigrant section of town, a brief walk away from Mount Royal, the mountain which divides the city and gives it its name. Every Sunday my father, with one or both children in tow, would stroll off to the Jewish Community Centre near Fletcher's Field and parade up and down, talking to acquaintances, making new ones, endlessly transacting business in that lingua franca of Yiddish – a truly democratic language which paid no attention to national borders, which could be spoken with any variation of accents or vowels with no stigma of class attached, perhaps because in its highest oral form it tumbled into German.

Money was a problem. By purveying flour and engaging in various manufacturing enterprises in Poland, my father had amassed enough in the immediate post-war period to keep his family in style, to pay for travel to France and eventually immigration to Canada. A bad business partnership in Paris had substantially shrunk the coffers. The nest-egg he thought he had accumulated with his New York brother had vanished, either in the latter's rash expenditure or in the legitimate business of procuring passports. Whatever the case, in that first year in Montréal, my father had to resort to peddling. He filled his beat-up secondhand Chevy, or maybe it was a Dodge, with God only knows what goods and went selling from door to door through the French-speaking northern and eastern suburbs of the city. No wonder the shipboard smile disappeared from his face and tempers were occasionally frayed.

Come September and I was sent off to school. I only remember a grey factory of a building and endless corridors. I don't remember any friends or teachers. I don't remember what language I spoke or whether I spoke at all, since my English – and the school was certainly English – couldn't have been altogether up to scratch. My mother, whose stories until she reached the hoary age of perpetual complaint, were always success stories, claims the headmaster told her I was far too advanced for kindergarten and had to be upgraded into the first year. I don't know.

SCENES OF MEMORY   19

All I remember is sitting at the bottom of that steep outdoor staircase and waiting for my mother to come home from her job, at the local Jewish library she says, and let me in. My keenest memories of childhood are of waiting – waiting outside in the heat or the cold or by a window, scratching the frost away in order to spy the passing cars – forcing my mind not to wait, distracting myself to no purpose, waiting in an agony of waiting for my parents to return. I am still a fretful waiter. I have never been able to maintain relations with a man who makes me wait. Five minutes will just about do. Ten and I have started pacing. Fifteen and the cold sweat begins. Twenty and I imagine abandonment, car crashes, a mounting spiral of disasters. I suspect my parents infected me with their wartime anxieties of waiting, an active, fitful waiting which can spill over into panic: waiting for the knock of the Gestapo at the door; waiting for absent loved ones at a time when every foray into the streets was an invitation to the disaster of deportation; endlessly waiting for those who would never return. My reality and my parents' wartime realities are worlds apart. But psychic states float about in families and can land wherever there's space for them.

Inside, the second-floor apartment was dark and warm, a warren of rooms with big, round, trailing ceiling pipes carrying heat against the Canadian winter from the fat metal stove. A lodger lived in the room at the front. Or perhaps we were her lodgers. It isn't clear. She was an old, grey-haired woman with a damp, unsmiling face. She rarely spoke and she smelled. Her only redeeming feature was her cat, a plump,

surly creature I loved, but who always evaded my arms and
rushed to hide under her bed. One day I broke the territorial
rules of the house and plunged after the tabby. I found myself
at the very source of the pong, a rank and dusty and turd-
infested nether region, hidden by drooping bedclothes. I
was wary of the cat after that. But I watched her. The funny
thing about her was that she didn't seem to mind waiting.
She would sit for hours in one corner or another by the
discoloured wall, her posture alert, expectant. 'Waiting for
mice,' my brother told me. His tone was always authoritative. 'Waiting to kill.'

   I guess waiting is no problem if you know who's the
stronger.

The main activity in the apartment took place around the
squat-legged stove. That was where the wooden rectangle of a
kitchen table stood. When it was covered with a white cloth,
embroidered with threads which gave off a slight sheen, my
parents' growing circle of friends gathered. The cloth and
others like it had made the journey from Poland, along with
two goose-down quilts, plump and slippery, just right for
snuggling. Their starched white covers had come too and
through the lozenge gap in their centre, the gold satin of the
quilts proudly announced itself. I don't know what expecta-
tions my parents had of the New World, but they had
evidently packed like fearful brides anticipating a stern and
taxing husband. The mollifying dowry included not only luxurious quilts and linen, but a dozen settings of ornately heavy
silver, embossed glasses, gold-rimmed china, complete with

vast soup tureens and curving ladles, plus my mother's capacious tawny pelisse. One could chart the entire history of my parents' slow metamorphosis into Canadians by the displacement of these objects. Each banishment to a remote top shelf, each replacement of duvet by plain woollen blanket and flowery sheets, silver by stainless steel, china by pottery or plastic, white linen by Formica, marked another notch in their becoming Canadian, until at last the fur-lined coat itself disappeared. Many years on, it was the children or the grandchildren who unearthed the remains of these exotic objects and dusted them off for use or display.

In the early days, when white linen still reigned in the dining room, the guests took their tea in tall glasses. Silver tongs released sparkling cubes of sugar into honey-gold liquid where a slice of lemon delicately floated. A crystal carafe poured out pungent measures of schnapps. But the voices of the 'friends' who sipped the tea or bolted down the schnapps bore none of the nostalgia which has unwittingly crept into my prose. Nostalgia is a wish effect, spurred in part by the objects of childhood, induced, mostly, by the imposing of narrative on distant memory. It is not inherent to the scene. The voices were often loud and argumentative. They battled over business or incomprehensible politics, grew low with gossip or unseemly jokes. They came in a babble of tongues. A sentence would begin in Polish, merge into Yiddish, migrate into French or stumbling English and go back again with no pause for breath.

The voices all told stories. There were so many stories in that first block of Canadian years, I no longer remember which faces belong to which. Their tellers are a blur which stretches into my early adolescence, their identities a jumble of features and haphazard occupations and business schemes. There were tailors and furriers and accountants and one-time doctors and almost-dentists. There was a man with a lined, ugly, pallid face in which intense eyes burned between red rims. There was a tiny woman with pink cherub cheeks and a giggling laugh. There was another with long hair and limbs and languid gestures. She wore rings and one ringed hand would always play over her inner arm where the tracery of blue numbers was etched. There was a gnome of a man with a dark mop of hair. When his head was bent next to my father's shiny pate, the thatch looked so like a wig, that it felt as if one quick gesture could achieve a desired transposition. There was a man with twinkling eyes married to a plump woman who never spoke, but ate unceasingly. Everyone ate – fragrant chicken soup with barley, sour-cream-flecked borscht with a hot potato at its centre, pickled herring buried in onion rings, slabs of boiled beef as thick as the moist bread, pastries filled with cinnamon and raisins or a sugary goo of apple. The ardour with which they ate spoke of an unstoppable hunger, as if food were a novelty which might disappear at any moment. So they ate and told stories.

The stories were repeated, amplified, changed for each new listener or each new occasion. Their common point was that they had nothing to do with the here and now. They were about another time and distant places. Strange names popped up in them. Grodzisk and Pruszków and Bialystok, Sverdlovskaya

Oblast and Stalin and Samarkand, Auschwitz and Treblinka and Nazis and Communists and Verflüchtehitler, which it took me a while to unravel into its component parts of 'Damned Hitler'. In my mind's eye the stories blend into one another and merge into a mysterious tapestry of war.

There is the story of my mother's best friend, blown up on the first day of the war by a single random bomb which hit the central village square, site of the well from which all water was daily fetched. She was the only person to be killed. 'And on the very first day,' the voices say with a touch of wonder.

There is the story of the man, holed up with some twenty others in a bunker in the midst of a freezing birch forest. For a while, food arrives and then suddenly it stops and one by one the inhabitants go off into the darkness to forage and are never seen again. Somewhere in this story, there are guns and battles between initials whose meaning I don't know.

There are the stories of walking, forth and back, from one village or town to another – a mad, gruelling geography of pursuit and escape, of distant cousins and aunts offering a night's shelter, of a search for safe harbours, of rivers crossed and bribed boatmen and cold, cold winters into which people vanish.

There are stories of tiny, overcrowded rooms, barricaded behind wardrobes, of darkness and whispers and shared breadcrusts.

There are stories of bartering and the meanness of peasants, of a watch exchanged for two eggs, of a gold necklace for a small sack of potatoes. As if to counter them, there are stories of generosity, of poor meals shared in bare houses, of a straw bed and a bowl of milk in a lonely barn. Value is a matter of need, someone grunts.

Trains feature prominently in these stories. There is the German section and the Polish section. They move fitfully in heaves and starts or don't move at all. They are the sites of punch-ups or fearsome inspections by uniformed men. Sometimes they are hideously crowded and have no windows and children scream.

The worst stories are told obliquely, in hushed voices, usually when their principal subject has left the room. 'They operated on her, you know. One of their crazy experiments. She can't now. No children.' But when the woman with the blue jottings on her arm comes back into the room, she is smiling. And everyone else smiles too.

It was only retrospectively that I understood that these stories were poignant, often tragic. The emotion of their telling was something else – a matter-of-factness which lightly cloaked a bristling excitement. The excitement of triumph. These were stories of heroism, of Herculean feats or Odyssean wiliness, tales of escape, of happy-enough-endings, of amazing good fortune, sometimes of miracles. No one ever used the word 'survivor', with its grim underpinnings of guilt and victim-hood and aura of everlasting misery. I don't think anyone felt guilty about having made it through. Maybe guilt is something one feels in situations of utter passivity, and these people had all acted. Survivor was a word then reserved for those who had come out of natural disasters. This was a man-made one, a piece of history which had not yet acquired the political freight of the word Holocaust. Nor had the current discourse of trauma and its effects yet arrived on the scene. That had to wait for Vietnam and a burgeoning therapeutic industry. My parents and their friends only talked of their great good luck. If the baggage they carried with them was weighty with loss, they were still prepared to trade it in for the future. History was something one left behind, something to be endlessly repeated only in stories. And in these, pain, the leaping of barbaric hurdles, was metamorphosed into triumph. The worst, apart from the evocation of names, was left to silence. The implicit message was that you could live through terrible things and come out at the other end to sip a glass of tea or schnapps.

In a sense, these were my childhood fairytales – hideous trajectories, skilfully navigated towards some kind of happy ever after. No one bothered with Grimm. But at the age when I had grown out of fairytales, they persisted. Bored with the repetition, I would go off and lie on the sofa and read the less loaded adventures of the Bobbsey Twins or Nancy Drew. I didn't realise then that the repetition was necessary. Not until the stories had been voided of their quantum of fear and pain, could they cease. I guess that took until I was about thirteen.

None the less, well into my teens and even later, whenever my parents made new friends, the stories were dusted off and brought out again, now with the Canadian utensils. Everyone always had a story of past suffering, of distant origins and arrival. Sharing it was a way of grounding the other. Only when I landed in Britain as a graduate student, did it come to me that not all people told their entire life's history on a first meeting. Only immigrants do that. When your roots are long and deep and safely earthed in the back garden with the roses, there's no need. Then it may be insulting or an invasion of privacy to probe.

Lying

Sometime in 1952, we moved to Ste-Thérèse-de-Blainville, a small town with a large church, some sixty miles north of Montréal. My parents had taken up the opportunity of leasing a shop on the main street. Amongst other more immediately practical matters, it was also an opportunity for repetition.

Like so many small towns in the province of Québec, Ste-Thérèse was then and still is ninety-nine per cent French-speaking. In the fifties, this meant it was also altogether Catholic. The church hierarchy dominated the town as surely as its sparkling aluminium-clad steeple towered over the flat countryside. From the church precinct with its grey stone seminary and adjacent convent buildings, the streets of the town spread in a haphazard arrangement of brick and clapboard houses. The High Street with its bank, police station, scattering of shops and single cinema, was a narrow, trailing artery, running the length of the town and abutting on to the highway. Employment was provided by a General Motors plant which assembled parts made in the United States, a plywood factory and a piano factory. The population was largely

working class. Families were vast: a triumph of agrarian and
Catholic values. Fifteen children to one mother and father
were not uncommon. It was the kind of town where at the age
of eighteen, girls had all their teeth removed in order to
acquire a false set.

My parents' store, deep and squat, bore the name 'Au Bon
Marché', whether as a signal of the cheapness of the goods
within or as a desiring wave towards its grand Parisian kin, no
one ever explained. The shop sat between a garage and a cinema.
Its assortment of dry goods had to compete with shining Chevys
and gas pumps and particularly on Fridays, late-opening night,
with John Wayne, Clark Gable, Rita Hayworth or Marilyn
Monroe. The range of clothes sold seemed as various as the films
we children – by Québec and therefore Catholic law – were not
permitted to see. There were long johns and thick windbreak-
ers and boots suitable for icy days on the range, lacy bras in
mysterious sizes and sequinned dresses and red high-heeled slip-
pers just like those in the film posters next door. Depending on
the season, there were also padded snowsuits or chequered halter
tops, twirling skirts in thick wool or khaki shorts. And there
were always nylons and cotton socks and stockings, unpackaged
in those days, stacked in neat, slightly musty piles in white cardboard boxes behind a counter.

After school or on Saturdays, I was most often to be found
stacked beneath a neighbouring counter. Stretched out on a
bedding of brown paper bags, a book or doodling pad in my
hand, I would hide from customers and the embarrassing sales
talk my father and especially my mother engaged in. Later,
when a glass-fronted cubicle was constructed at the very back

of the store, I would climb into its narrow silence, perch at the desk and spread my homework over the thick accounts ledgers which lay there. Between sums I would stare through the pane at the strangely soundless spectacle of the shop, the customers moving like puppets between racks of clothes, eerily akin to the wigged mannequins in the window displays. Those mannequins – with their bright unwavering eyes beneath brush-like lashes, their 'skin' smoothly cold to the touch when they were dressed or undressed – terrified me. They had an odd crack around their waists. Their arms slotted off and on. In the corner of the cubicle two of these spare arms lay on the floor amidst an assortment of wigs. I always made sure they were covered. I hated dolls. When my parents talked of the dead, I imagined them like those mannequins with their severed bloodless limbs, their shaved hair, like that of death-camp inmates, woven into the silk of Nazi parachutes.

We had our own house now, a brief walk away from the store and left into a leafy street. It had a patch of grass in front, a wide wooden porch two steps up and a smooth rail all round made for climbing and jumping. In one of my first Canadian pictures, I am poised on that rail, my clothes a ludicrous assortment of checks and stripes, a vast white ribbon at my brow. The ribbon is distinctly foreign. It adorns all my photographs up to the age of eight except for my favourite. That one has me in the midst of Fletcher's Field in Montréal. I hold up the edges of my flowered frock and curtsey – the curtsey too is there in an assortment of early photos, a learned and appeasing gesture directed at the adult world. I am a good girl. I do not look unhappy. I always smile. Only when my brother enters the picture and presses down on my shoulders with visible force does the smile vanish.

I remember very little of my brother from my early childhood. The six-and-a-half years between us created a vast distance – a gap of war, as well as age and character. As I grew, my sense of him was of a commanding, indeed bullying presence. I would run into the bathroom and lock the door to get away from his booming orders and erratic blows. During his teenage years, when his rows with our parents proliferated, I would try to function as peacemaker. Or simply try to distract everyone's attention from the battle in progress. I don't think I was particularly successful, though I persisted. I hated the noise and the anger and the sense of danger which always seemed to accompany it.

But my brother was not around much in Ste-Thérèse. Unusually for Canada, he was boarding – not at a school, but with a family in Montréal – and preparing for high school as well as that ritual passage into manhood which is a Bar Mitzvah. It was not a manhood Catholic Ste-Thérèse provided. Nor was it one, it seems, he was prepared to enter. The Montréal rabbi claimed he was untutorable, unwilling to learn the requisite religious matter or abide by the rules. The Bar Mitzvah never took place.

Many years passed before I realised that this ambivalence about Jewishness, rarely spoken, yet acted out, was one of the many legacies of my parents' war years.

Inside, our house had the rambling, empty feel of shoes echoing on floorboards. Perhaps it was just bigger and less peopled

than any of the others we had lived in. My only distinct
memory of it is waking up in the closet of my parents' bedroom and shivering with cold and confusion and a panic of
tears. Apparently I did a fair amount of sleepwalking in those
days. Maybe my sleep was looking for something familiar.

I don't know if the sleepwalking memory comes from before
or after the nuns paid my parents a visit. As a matter of course,
I had been sent to the convent school, the one closest to our
new home. I don't know how the nuns sussed out I wasn't quite
right. Maybe I wasn't learning my catechism adequately or
maybe I said something revealing in class. In any event, the
swish of black habits arrived at the house. Beneath the elaborate wimples, the faces were unsmiling. A conversation took
place I wasn't permitted to hear. Was there a demand for baptismal papers, a laying down of the strict laws of the land?

Whatever transpired, by the next week I was enrolled in
a new school – an English-language school. French schools
were for Catholics only. The Protestant School Board got all
the rest. My parents hadn't realised that church-dominated
Québec had little in common with republican France. Only
in the seventies did the Québecois wake to the fact that if
they wanted French to be kept alive in the province, it paid
to be non-denominational. The irony of all this is that the
French-speaking six-year-old I was grew into an English
speaker. French was battered out of me by a succession of
English-speaking teachers of Québecois who didn't like my
Parisian, and must have liked my piping corrections of their
French even less. For daring to make them, I was stood in
a variety of classroom corners, face to the wall, tears of

humiliation forced back. On one occasion, I had my palms lashed by ten strokes of the ruler. The teacher who administered the punishment was particularly large and though her name was Mrs White, her cheeks were brightly pink. Nor was it clear whether I was being punished for the sin of insubordination or the crime of foreign – and I still insisted, correct – French. Whichever the case, from then on until I reached my teens, I dutifully failed French, though we carried on speaking another version of it at home.

After the Ste-Thérèse convent, my new school was in the neighbouring village of Rosemère, an English-speaking zone of large comfortable country houses bordering the Rivière des Mille Îles. The classroom looked out on trees and countryside and contained three or four age groups. This must have made for excitement, since it is one of the few schools I recall with a distinct sensation of pleasure. The others – four more in Montréal by the time I reached the age of twelve – blur into a sequence of repeated dullness, punctuated only by those degrading periods spent standing in the corner. Yet somehow my report cards were good, though they commented on my exceptionally high absentee rate. My mother was always willing to sign a note testifying to the loose fact that her daughter hadn't been feeling well.

I don't remember anyone worrying that a change of school posed a particular difficulty for the child. Education was a good, and a necessity. Where one acquired it was an irrelevance. Adaptability was taken for granted, as were better than average grades. In the hierarchy of immigrant worries, discontinuity of schooling heralded no problems. Perhaps as a result, it produced none. Children are adept at picking up and integrating parental cues. Worry, in my family, clustered in areas which had nothing to do with education.

When we arrived in Ste-Thérèse my parents changed their name. They changed it from Borenstein to Borens, ostensibly for simplicity and business efficiency. In fact they dropped the tell-tale syllable for more complicated reasons. We were Borenstein in cosmopolitan Montréal and Borens in the provincial reaches of Ste-Thérèse where Jews were rumours – disembodied myths of foul doings, school-ground Christ-killers, always spoken of in the expletive voice and coupled with the adjective dirty, so that two words became one: 'saljuif!' I suspect we were the only embodied Jews in Ste-Thérèse, though there may have been others who behaved with equal secrecy.

My parents had a history of name-changing. During the war, they lived under a succession of 'Aryan' aliases, changing names and identities and addresses when discovery was imminent, precariously acquiring documents and baptismal certificates as need demanded. One or other of them was variously Sawitzka, Kowalski, Zabłocki, with the necessary preceding saints' names to match. In Ste-Thérèse they found it expedient to keep up the habit of double identity.

For all its accessible comforts, the brave new post-war world of Québec was hardly a region where Jews were welcome. In the fifties the Québecois – mostly Church-ruled farmers – still nourished their prejudices as assiduously as their kindred Poles and, given the far smaller proportion of Jewish inhabitants, with far less reason. From 1933, the moment that Hitler's actions against

Jews resulted in a first wave of immigrants, until 1948, when the
creation of Israel helped to empty the post-war refugee camps of
the surviving Jews, whom few countries wanted to allow through
their doors, Canada practised a highly discriminatory immigration policy. Jews were undesirables, occasionally to be pitied at
a distance, rarely to be allowed the privilege of entry. At the
height of the war, when there was talk of just under one hundred
Iberian-based refugees coming into Canada, Maurice Duplessis,
long-time premier of Québec, ran a cynical election campaign
claiming that 100,000 Jews were poised to flood Québec with
the help of the Liberal government in Ottawa, in cahoots with
an International Zionist Brotherhood. Needless to say, the Jews
who had made it to the comparative safety of the Iberian
Peninsula never reached Canada.

Nor was anti-Semitism, in the fifties, limited to small-town,
Catholic Québec. Under a veneer of gentility and Protestant
tolerance, Montréal WASPS practised a similar bigotry. In my
childhood, scores of tennis and country clubs were closed to
Jews, as was property in Westmount, that exclusive part of the
city which flanks one extensive side of the mountain. To be fair,
Westmount was also closed to French Canadians. In the
divided city which Montréal then was, WASPS occupied the
peaks which the Jews gradually infiltrated and the Québecois
finally stormed.

I don't know whether it was chance or choice which led my
parents to Ste-Thérèse – probably a mixture of the two. In
either event, the duplicities learned in war persisted. Not that
I was consciously aware of their origin. All I knew was that at
home we were Jewish and in the town we weren't. If none of

this was altogether spelled out, every outing still necessitated a rehearsal of what could and couldn't be said to whom. Things grew curiouser and curiouser. And troubling.

Every family has its division of psychological labour. In mine, my mother was the liar, my father the silent, inscrutable one, while I was the truthteller. Or at least, the truthknower. In my fantasy of my childhood self, I rarely speak. I am a quiet girl who keeps her own counsel. My much absent brother is mysterious and unpredictable. As he had been very close to my mother during the war, he may have found the Machiavellian slippage between truth and fiction altogether unsurprising.

From my little girl's vantage point, my mother was a fantastic spinner of intricate webs. There were no straightforward human transactions. If I was sent out to the shop for a bottle of milk, it was never a simple expedition. I was to tell the shopkeeper that my mother was very sorry not to come herself, but she had had to go to the doctor or the dentist or was detained by urgent business. And I was to ask after his wife or children. When we saw one friend or another in Montréal, I was never to say that we had seen X or Y the week before, but simply mention Z. Meanwhile, I would listen to my mother recounting elaborate fictions about our visit with Z or narratives of my school doings which zoomed off into a stratosphere that bore no relation to mundane facts. Even the weather needed a gloss. Where we had been on the weekend, the sun always shone, or the rain poured down interminably – depending on whom we were talking to.

Sometimes her confabulations grew so rich that she forgot

certain portions of them and the lying peeped through. Increasingly, with time, I would catch her out and rebuke her, but she would simply carry on, without missing a breath. Or if we were alone, look at me with her wide-set eyes of innocent blue and declare with an emphasis, chilling in its sincerity, that she only ever told the truth. Occasionally my father would shake his head and mutter 'diplomat' or make a scabrous Polish pun on the word, which rendered it 'shitomat'.

Indeed, from one perspective, my mother's fictions were acts of star quality diplomacy, a manipulation of human events aimed at a kind of social peace or place. There was no particular malice in them. Everything had only to be seen in the best possible social light. Facts could be nipped and tucked or even invented to arrive at this bright aim. My father and I took on the silent complicity of an audience watching a performance everyone else considered an ordinary encounter. If he saw me tense, poised to interrupt, he would wink and make a barely perceptible shaking gesture. He never contradicted her in public, never gainsaid her. Perhaps his increasing silence was based on a fear of exposing her, simply by forgetting the network of little lies.

When I had my own children, I recognised the harsh literalness of their social imagination. For them, even the lies which oil the great machine of society are utterly unacceptable. My daughter will interrupt or give me a scathing look if I tell the white lie which rescues someone's feelings. 'No, you got that letter three days ago, Mum. Not today,' she will announce in a loud voice, as I attempt an operation which saves someone's face or my own. So I have paused over my childhood and wondered whether my mother's fabulations, so difficult to come to terms with, were simply those inevitable white lies all grown-ups engage in. Yet it seems to me that her fictions did have an urgent undertow and a boundlessness which transported them into another category. For instance when I was eighteen and moved out of the house, it took her years to tell anyone, so that I had to return phone calls as if I were at home and if anyone then asked to speak to my mother, I, too, would be forced to lie and say she wasn't in. (Coward that I was – or simply conditioned to family loyalty – I never exposed her to any of her friends.) Years passed before she told some of her circle that I was married, since I had married out of the clan; and then longer still to declare me divorced.

Some of these controlling maternal fictions are not unusual. Others of my mother's distinctly were.

Not only were we not Jewish in Ste-Thérèse and other select venues, not only did we have different names in different places, but we also acquired a new set of origins. At home, while I was still in the smaller single digits, I thought I knew I had been born in Poland. Out on the street, a threshold of several thousand kilometres had been crossed, and I was suddenly a 'petite Parisienne', born in France, like my mother. My father didn't qualify – perhaps because his French didn't sparkle with the same accent. This fiction of birth, with all the necessary attendant frills, was trotted out not only for potential anti-Semites, but increasingly for all and sundry. I think it even appeared on some school records.

Truth is a slippery substance and it can easily slip away in a kind of familial osmosis. I got to the point where I was no longer sure where I had been born – one isn't after all really present at one's own birth. And origins are the very stuff of myth. Well into my teens, I remember going into a kind of shivering panic when asked my name, but especially when I was asked my place of birth. The question paralysed me. I staged elaborate ploys to prevent its arrival or avoid an answer. Nor did I know what answer would come out of me. Even when I told what I supposed was the truth, I had a shuddering sense that I was probably lying.

During the war, my parents had been forced to reinvent themselves at various strategic turns. They lived by their wits and they lied to survive. The best liars got through best of all. There were no rules and what rules there were existed to be broken. They had, after all, been created by a killing regime solely in its own interest. As George Soros, who was a young man in wartime Hungary, says of his father, 'He realised that the normal rules did not apply. Obeying the law became a dangerous addiction; flouting it was the way to survive.'

My mother, according to family legend, was the best flouter of rules and teller of lies. In mid-war and by the age of twenty-seven (if that was her age), Hena or Hania or Henriette had been through at least three different personae, none of them Jewish. She had invented parts and pasts for her various identities, had schooled my infant brother and her own terrified mother in theirs, had worked in offices under the steely eyes of officials, had confabulated my father out of various precarious situations. Had become a heroine. Whatever horrendous baggage the war brought with it, it was also the most exciting time of her life – a time which retrospectively and even if only in the telling gave her a greater sense of power than any subsequent years. So she recreated what she had lived and learned there, though it was not altogether appropriate in the calm expanse of Canada. Like some lead actress in love with her part, she carried on playing off-stage, rehearsed her family in secondary roles, tried to control their destinies. If she didn't succeed, the failure never quite entered her mind or at least, her fictions. These carry on into the present. Their content has lost its sense, but the form is intact: a wandering, drifting narrative which gathers stray details into itself, meanders into other stories, loses truth in a loquacity which dizzies the listener, makes him forget solid ground, while all the while attempting to seduce.

My mother's ideal interlocutor is always and ever the Gestapo officer.

Though I didn't realise it for many years, the choice or chance of Québec was fortuitous, certainly for my mother. People need to escape but they also need to bring their habits with them or they have no psychological ammunition with which to function in the world. Québec was familiar to my parents. In certain ways, its small-town conditions mirrored those of Poland. Catholic anti-Semitism was rife in both. The social stratification was the same: a powerful clergy, small middle class, and a conservative agrarian population just moving into industrialisation. Feared as a mass, the individuals in this population were from my mother's point of view, still simple and good. They were also objects of contempt – too simple, not on a par with the cultivated Jews. Like Polish peasants, they could be both wooed and manipulated. My mother spoke in the

same terms and same tone of voice about both. And she carried
on wooing, manipulating and lying – out of expediency and
because it provided that triumphant electric charge of risk sur-
mounted.

For a child, lying opens the window on a double world.
Ambiguities and ambivalence fly in, like so many bats to roost
in one's hair. Lying implies there is something to hide either out
there or in here. In my case, the secret was tainted origins.
Poland was a bad place, a shadowy region, not good enough to
foster my birth – otherwise why give it a French mask? But we
also lied about being Jews, so whatever the occasional aside or
riff illustrating superiority, Jewishness too carried a shameful
taint, one which had on too many occasions proved mortal.

On reflection it would have been surprising if the taint
hadn't been there. We all internalise the discourse of the master,
the coloniser, the aggressor. Jews, blacks, immigrants – all carry
within them that little nugget of self-hatred, the gift of the
dominant culture to its 'lesser' mortals. At times, the nugget is
dusted off, polished into brilliance, transformed into pride,
brandished on communal occasions. But it rarely altogether
dissolves. And it retains a bitter aura of shame.

Blonde and Dark

As I grew into my teens, so did my nose. It seemed far more precarious an appendage than my breasts. It arched at the top and drooped slightly at the bottom. I would spend hours in front of the mirror, doggedly gazing at this ghastly protuberance from different perspectives – full frontal, in profile, head lifted or bent. Raising it at the arch with finger or pencil resulted in a marked improvement, but then my nostrils gaped, two dizzying black holes.

'Big nose!' my brother jeered helpfully at every occasion when our paths crossed – which was now too often for my liking, since we had moved in quick succession to a Montréal apartment and then a house in the suburbs.

'You look just like your father,' parental friends commented and received quick acquiescence from my mother.

I grimaced and protested inwardly. I didn't look like my father. I had a ton of dark hair where he had none. The shapes of our faces were different. Nor did I have to shave mine.

And yet, it was quite clear that I didn't look like my mother. She was (and still is) a blonde. A beautiful honey-blonde, to boot, with deep-set blue eyes where mine are muddy brown, a perfect nose with just a tiny turn-up at the tip – like my brother's – wonderful cheekbones and chiselled chin. My mother's beauty was both legendary and actual. Everyone paid tribute to it. Marlene Dietrich was mooted as a comparison. Or Zsa Zsa Gabor. Men with throaty voices rang her up and rang again and again. She would stand in the back room of what was by now a second and became a third in a small chain of stores, tap her fingers innocently, and listen to hours of sweet nothings being poured into her ear.

But it was the blondeness and its attendant nose that mattered.

Her family had been fair, my father's dark. My maternal grandfather – a rabbi and teacher – had had a long and full blond beard, and was hailed locally as *'der gaele Rebbe'*, the blond rabbi. My maternal grandmother, too, was fair. My mother's brother, whose epic heroism soared above the family circle, was the blondest of all; 'blonder-than-any-German' was the usual epithet.

My own brother, by virtue of his nose and early blondness, was marked out for the glorious maternal line. I was relegated to the nether realms of dark paternity. Not that I wasn't told I was pretty and clever and all those things good-enough parents tell their children, but I knew, none the less, that I belonged down there with the darkies.

In my mother's oft-repeated narrative of her pre-war life, blondeness recurs as an important feature. It is a talisman bestowed by generally jealous gods. To be blond is to be favoured. This is not of course an aberration peculiar to her. From Botticelli's Venus to Goldilocks to Marilyn Monroe, blondes, as we all know, have more fun. But my mother's story bears a particular inflection.

She grew up in Grodzisk Mazowiecki, a small town thirty-two kilometres south-west of Warsaw. In the 1930s the town's population numbered about 11,000 of which a quarter were Jewish – though since the total population figure includes the peasantry in the surrounding countryside, the centre of Grodzisk was in fact about seventy per cent Jewish. Her parents, David and Sara Lipszyc had moved there just after the First World War from Serokomla, a village in the vicinity of Lublin about one hundred kilometres from the Belorus border. They already had their two children: Adek who was born in 1911 and my mother, Hena, born on December 24, 1915 – or so the story goes.

On a recent visit from Montréal, where he lives and runs an art gallery, my brother told me a story about our Lipszyc grandfather that no longer appears in my mother's reduced memory. He told it in an excited and proud voice, as if he were once again a small boy alive to legends of ancestral bravura. During the early years of the First World War, David Lipszyc had served as a captain in the Uhlans, a light cavalry regiment. His men adored him despite his Jewishness. When he was buried beneath a collapsed trench during an artillery barrage, they risked their lives to search for him. The tip of a spur jutting out of the ground provided a trace. The men dug, found a wounded David and defiantly carried him home. At the end of the war, they returned to present him with an inscribed pocket watch and a ruby ring. Both of these David Lipszyc later gave to his infant grandson, my brother, who promptly dismantled the watch and was unable to reassemble it. The ruby ring disappeared during the Warsaw Uprising.

David Lipszyc had studied in Warsaw before the First World War and become involved with one of the mainstream Jewish political parties, the Mizrahi. Immediately after the war, he was sent to Grodzisk under the party's aegis to set up an elementary school. Things were changing rapidly in Poland at the time and he was caught up in the new spirit of modernity. The country was at last independent after 136 years of occupation. Political groupings of all colours, both religious and secular, sprang up and vanished overnight. These defied any routine demarcations between left and right, Jewish and Polish. Everyone argued exuberantly: what kind of Jew might one be in this new Poland? Urban and secular? Orthodox or socialist and Zionist? And what constituted Jewishness if religion was no longer an absolute imperative? Was one a Polish Jew or a Jewish Pole?

Education too was in flux. Radical pedagogical ideas arrived from Vienna. People disputed the value of the traditional small-town, one-room *heder*, or Jewish elementary school, with its impoverished dictatorial teacher and rote learning for boys only. The pace of change increased when the Polish government introduced a law insisting on a secular component within Jewish education.

Though a religious man, David Lipszyc was also a progressive. The school he set up was a *heder metukkan*, a new improved *heder*, which incorporated contemporary educational ideas. Hebrew was taught in Hebrew and thus spoken, rather than limited to prayer, as orthodox law insists. No one was beaten. Unusually, too, children were taught from the first to read and write in Polish. On top of that, there were classes in history and mathematics. David Lipszyc himself taught maths and Hebrew. Accounts from my mother's two surviving Grodzisk friends shore up her narrative of a community in which her father was a highly respected elder, a giant of a man sought out for his Talmudic as well as practical wisdom, a democrat who paid little heed to hierarchy. And yes, blond.

In small-town or *shtetl* terms, the family occupied a presti-gious position. They were comfortable, if not wealthy – though comfort and wealth are relative terms. Grodzisk, unlike say Łódź, with its famous industrialists, was not a site of Jewish luxury. The family apartment on the second floor of a house made of stone (not of the more common wood), stood near the school and on the same street as the synagogue. The flat num-bered three rooms. A courtyard toilet served the entire building. Water had to be fetched from the well in the central square. In winter, this square was iced over and fetching water involved acrobatic skill. Those who lived at a distance from the well brought two buckets with them, balanced by a bar across the shoulders. For the poor, the widowed and the ill, food was scarce; access to warm clothes and basic medicine even scarcer. A friend of my mother's remembers walking barefoot in summer to conserve the shoes essential in winter; during the Passover festival, the community provided the unleavened bread, the *matzohs* which ritual demands, since his family of four children and a widowed mother couldn't afford this extra expense.

In my mother's family, shoes were worn all year round and
no one went hungry. Sara Lipszyc was a traditionalist, a good
cook and a stringent housekeeper. She adhered to all the rules
and rituals orthodox Jewish law prescribes to women. Her
blonde hair was covered by a wig and her face devoid of makeup. In preparation for the Sabbath, she washed and scrubbed
and attired the house, baked the woven white loaves or *chal-
lahs*, cooked stuffed, sweetened carp and boiled beef, as well as
that slow-simmering stew, the *cholent*, put in the oven the day
before so that no fires need be lit on the holy day. She made the
blessings and said her prayers assiduously, far more so, it seems,
than her husband. She also rigorously ensured that her family
was well fed and with equal rigour, that her men had time for
their all-important learning. Her place was assigned. She was
a respected, a loved, but also a lesser being. Indeed, in my
mother's memory, her own mother has crystallised into the
shtetl woman of legend – the perfect, anxious housekeeper, who
sends her daughter scurrying off to her son's school with a
lunch pail, in order to ensure that her all-important boy, her
eldest by four-and-a-half years, doesn't go hungry.

One of the few stories about Sara that has passed into family
myth tells of her courtship, way back somewhere around 1910.
My mother always narrates this story from my grandfather's
point of view, so it must have come from him, and it thus takes
on something of the significance of a parable – one that still
makes her wonder.

David had spied Sara on one of his passages through
Serokomla. He couldn't of course approach her himself, so the
local matchmaker was asked to arrange a meeting. Rather than

donning her Sabbath best for this important and formal first encounter with her suitor, Sara appeared in her everyday apron. Perplexed, David queried this unusual modesty and asked whether, perhaps, she wasn't interested in a match. 'No, no,' Sara replied. 'But I don't want to pretend to be something I'm not. What you see today is what you'll get.'

Her daughter certainly didn't inherit the maternal line on appearances. Nor, from her own account, on much else. Indeed, when my mother wants to pay me one of her ambivalent compliments, she tells me that I must have my grandmother's genes. Cooking genes, to be exact. She, herself, apart from the annual creation of a pot of stuffed carp, *gefilte fish*, has never cooked.

But it is David, her father, who looms largest in my mother's memory. She tells stories of his wisdom, his fairness, his egalitarianism, his lack of prejudice, his modern outlook. 'A tailor can be as good a man as a scholar,' she quotes him as saying – a statement which utterly defies the Jewish convention of putting Talmudic scholarship above all else. When she talks of him, there is always something about her of the reverent four-year-old in love with Daddy. It was this Daddy who taught my mother always to tell the truth. This perhaps explains her own oft-repeated claim that she does so, contrary to all evidence. Truth comes with a double paternal sanction – secular and religious. The first Hebrew characters Jewish children are taught are those which spell out the word truth – *emet*.

By special dispensation, my mother was the only girl in an all-boy school. A quick learner, she eventually went on to *gymnasium* and teacher-training college in Warsaw – an hour's train ride away given stops in numerous towns, including Pruszków where my father lived. She was also by all reports, the belle of the community, a flirt and a tease, the object of every boy's eye. Her entire lunch money, scrupulously saved over months, went into the frivolity of a much desired pink scarf spied in a Warsaw shop window. The scarf has stayed in a mind where so much else has disappeared, perhaps because of the fierce maternal disapproval its covert purchase elicited. 'Where did the money come from?' Sara grilled her when Hena accidentally wore the secret scarf in front of her one day. Hena gulped and hedged and explained to a disbelieving Sara that her lunch money was far too generous, so she had been able to save. Only paternal intervention allowed the scarf to be kept.

The single surviving photograph of my mother in her teenage years shows her booted and trousered, cycling along a narrow lane, her blondeness less in evidence than her shyly satisfied smile of independence. Despite the dilapidated houses and wooden cart behind her, there is nothing of the modesty of the *shtetl* woman in her direct gaze. A boy stares after her. He may be one of the mischievous youths who banded together to cover her face in a wet white cloth in order to test whether her perfect complexion came out of a bottle or was her own. Hena passed the test: her complexion, ever after, remained a subject of primary interest.

The bicycle she rides in the photograph is a man's and has large inverted handlebars. It may belong to her brother Adek, who encouraged her to ride and climb and be fearless. He also slipped her extra pocket money to go to the movies. But judging by Hena's age in the picture, her adored elder brother had already left Grodzisk either to do his military service or for university. Though it made their pious mother quake, Adek was adamantly secular. Destined for a professional life, he was also something of an adventurer and from all accounts, a ladies' man.

'The girls wept over him,' my mother still says happily. 'He was so handsome. Especially in his uniform. I had to comfort a whole line of broken hearts.'

It was Adek who introduced Hena to my father. Both men were members of Bethar, a young militaristic Zionist group, the party of the charismatic Vladimir Jabotinski, which took a non-pacifist line on the founding of a Jewish state. Such groups met across Poland to debate tactics and future, attend lectures, engage in bodybuilding sports and train for what they believed would be necessary battle. Whereas my mother's family thoroughly approved of Aron, on my father's side there were hurdles to be crossed. My paternal grandmother, Estera Borensztejn, a robust matriarch who, apart from having raised eight children, ran the extensive family business with an iron hand, had heard rumours that my father was frequenting that forbidden object, a *shiksa* – a Gentile woman.

'Not enough Jewish girls in town?' she rebuked him. 'You have to dig out a *shiksa*.'

'You'll see when you meet her,' my father-in-love smiled.

The meeting didn't achieve the desired effect. Estera Borensztejn was still not convinced of my blonde mother's necessary Jewishness. She had to gather her considerable girth and make the journey to Grodzisk to interview my mother's parents. Only then, at the sight of the rabbinical beard, was she wholly satisfied of her soon to be daughter-in-law's Jewish origins.

My mother has told this story over and over again across the years. It is one of the few of her accounts which has survived unchanged into her old age. It is etched firmly in her slippery memory – a touchstone of glee and glory.

As a child, I never quite understood why she should take such pride in being mistaken for a *shiksa*. In fact, this story, like other references to her beaux and good looks, always made dark little me feel somewhat queasy. Not until recently, when I immersed myself in some of the complexities of Jewish–Gentile relations in Poland, did I begin to fathom her particular pleasure in being blonde. The reading carried me way back in time to the medieval origins of the *shtetl* in whose latter days my mother had spent her formative years. Ignorant as I was and shaped within the retrospective pall the Holocaust has cast over Polish-Jewish history, much of what I discovered surprised me.

Poles and Jews had lived side by side within those floating borders we now call Poland since the twelfth century. Welcomed as a class of necessary traders in what was primarily an agricultural country, Jews were granted privileges far greater than anywhere else in Europe. As early as 1264 – at the very time when Jews were being hounded out of England by punitive laws and taxes – the Statute of Kalisz forbade discrimination in court and guaranteed full protection of life and property to new Jewish settlers. Jews could practise their own religion, as well as the professions. Gradually the country became a populous centre of Jewish life. In 1576, the reforming king, Stefan

Batory, took things further. He banned the accusation of ritual murder, a traditional Catholic weapon of terror against Jews. Five years later, an unprecedented institution, the Jewish Council of the Four Lands, came into being and gave Polish Jews full religious and communal autonomy. The community prospered and became the largest Jewish settlement in the world. Jews, here, were not only merchants and artisans, brewers and distillers, millers and innkeepers, but because of the Polish aristocracy's disdain for commerce, they also rose to be estate and forestry managers and traders in rural produce.

As overseers of vast independent estates, Jews, however, were required to act as tax collectors, not a role calculated to endear them to a peasantry increasingly in thrall to a Church which damned Jews as enemy infidels. In effect the Polish state protected these useful Jews from the Church and from the envy and suspicion of difference which can so easily spill over into violence. Tolerated, if not loved, the Jews returned the favour: outside the world of work, they tended to keep to their own kind. Until the dissolution of the Council of the Four Lands in 1764, Poles and Jews thus co-existed as two separate but inextricably entangled nations – a multiculturalism before the word came into common use. Poland's 'Golden Age of Independence' was also a golden age for the Jews.

But with the civil and economic strife of the late eighteenth century came the progressive disintegration of a protective central authority. This put Jews in the firing line: a large-scale massacre took place in the town of Uman in 1768. Attacked from without and within, the Polish Kingdom fell apart. Between 1772 and 1795, Russia, Prussia and Austria divided up

the country and its one million Jews. Intolerance was now reinforced either by energetic assimilationist policies or legal
discrimination. The Poles too suffered at the hands of the occu-
piers, so much so that the great poet of Polish Romanticism,
Adam Mickiewicz, made Jews the image of Poland's own suffering and longing for independence.

With the growth of nineteenth-century nationalism and
pogroms – instigated by the Russians to cleanse the heartland
of all faiths but the orthodox – animosity between Poles and
Jews mounted. An increasingly anti-Semitic Polonism found its
mirror image in Zionism, the movement for a Jewish homeland. By the turn of the new century, extremist Poles wanted
the Jews to go and many Jews wanted to leave – if the necessary means and the necessary homeland presented itself. Both
sides complained of each other and were mystified by each
other – not only in terms of religious differences, but styles of
life.

Unlike the Jews of Western Europe, the majority of Polish
Jews maintained the customs which had consolidated into
'orthodoxy' in the seventeenth century, well into the first half
of the twentieth. They were a visible presence. Whatever his
liberal attitudes, my maternal grandfather wore the long black
coat, round, fur-trimmed hat and full beard, though not the
curling forelocks, of convention. At home and in the jostling
streets of the town, he largely spoke Yiddish. His food was
always kosher. Despite his stint in the army, he would have
declared himself in the 1931 census to be part of the 80 per cent
of Polish Jews who were unassimilated and considered Yiddish
to be their mother tongue. I imagine he would have included

himself in a similar percentage who thought themselves Jews by nationality. Certainly both he and my father read some of the 130 Yiddish and Hebrew periodicals which circulated in Poland. Though the families could name a few Polish friends, most of their relations were with other Jews.

The Great Depression put many such Polish-Jewish relations under severe strain. The right-wing and centre press called for immediate emigration of a substantial proportion of Poland's 3.3 million Jews. They pointed out that although Jews numbered some ten per cent of Poland's population, they comprised 21.5 per cent of the professional classes and about half of the country's doctors and lawyers. Even more significantly, Jewish firms employed over 40 per cent of the Polish urban labour force.

Influenced by their German neighbours, militant national-ist groups argued for a campaign of violence, including pogroms. In towns and small cities, where Jews constituted some thirty per cent or more of the population and owned the majority of shops and inns, the Poles made moves to boycott already hard-hit Jewish businesses. Peasant co-operatives bypassed Jewish merchants in the countryside and sold their produce only to Christians. With the death in 1935 of Jósef Pilsudski, Poland's great hero-liberator and sometime protec-tor of the Jews, things took a decided turn for the worse. Unassimilated Jews were barred from state employment. The sale of kosher meat was restricted and Sunday banned as a day of business. In small towns, like my mother's, anti-Semitic vio-lence erupted and in the universities Fascist groups provoked brawls. The *numerus clausus*, restricting the Jews to a limited percentage of university places, was imposed. In legal and medical faculties, a 'ghetto bench' for Jews came into being. In protest many Jews stood, instead of sitting, during lectures and were joined by those Poles who defied the anti-Semitic upsurge.

It was in these years of growing anti-Semitic agitation that my parents lived out their young adulthood. The small town of Grodzisk was a microcosm of Polish politics. There were Socialist Bundists with their red scarves, and extreme Polish nationalists and their counterparts, the militaristic Zionists, who paraded defiantly in equal and opposite action with sticks in their hands. Small Jewish tradesmen had their shops boycotted and attacked. Trains were dangerous places: gangs of thugs searched out Jews and flung them through the doors. Sundays, when the peasants came to church in town and doubled its population, were particularly precarious. One of the surviving family friends told me, 'As a child, when I walked in the street and saw a Pole coming up, I was always frightened. They would spit in your face, call you "dirty Jew" or jeer "Jews to Palestine". When they got drunk, any pretext was good enough for beating up a Jew. After church on Sundays, my mother wouldn't let me out of the house. We were always afraid of pogroms.' The same man, it should be noted, also told me he had a few good Polish friends, one of whom kept him company on the train so he wouldn't be attacked.

Though they had come from fairly traditional families, my parents were both 'Western' in their outlook. They were young, members of a new and energetic post-war generation. Their world, they felt, would be different from the conservative and oppressive *shtetl* sphere of their forebears. For one thing, they spoke and wrote good Polish. For another, they read 'secular' literature widely, gobbling up translations of foreign fiction as soon as they appeared. Somerset Maugham and Ilya Ehrenburg featured prominently on my mother's recollected list of favourites beside *Anna Karenina* and *Madame Bovary*. There was theatre, too, and an occasional visit to the opera to sit in the 'gods'. But above all, there were the movies. The taboo glamour of Rudolf Valentino played itself out on silent screens and emphatically on my mother, who remembers him far more vividly than much else and still flushes in coquettish delight at the mere mention of his name. And then, just as my mother was going through the formative years of her femininity, Marlene Dietrich burst on to the screens – a ready-made icon of blonde inviolability, all cool seduction and languid power, and German to boot.

My mother went to school in a particularly useful form of blondeness. All her friends, she claims, told her she was as like Marlene as a sister.

For my mother, being blonde was an easy path into assimilation. No overt incident of anti-Semitism directed at her took place in her young life before the war. When she left the confines of Grodzisk to get on the Warsaw train which took her to her grammar school, she was simply a young and attractive woman. Not that she ever consciously rejected her Jewishness or went through any kind of religious crisis. I don't believe that she ever confronted the Jewish question, as such. She could simply pass – pass as a *shiksa*, a Gentile woman. It was a surface operation: no surgery required. And passing was a good thing. It meant there was no need for fear. During the war, it was also a means of survival.

When in my rebellious years, I used to accuse my mother of crass superficiality – for always talking about people's looks, for taking so much trouble over her makeup, for ensuring there was never any grey in her hair, for examining my own appearance with a cool, unconscious precision that bordered on contempt – she never seemed to understand what I meant. Appearances for her were a matter of depth, a matter of life and death.

The logic of racism is a logic of appearances.

For my father, the dark one, that logic played itself out in a different way.

Every summer, once finances permitted, my parents would take a week's holiday. We would get in the car and drive along near-empty highways towards upstate New York or Vermont where mountains and fresh air and resort hotels beckoned. As we neared the southernmost tip of the province of Québec, my father's colour would begin to change. He would grow pale, then waxy white. Beads of perspiration would gather on his brow and the top of his head. His shoulders would tense into ramrod position. By the time we arrived at the border-crossing, he was incapable of speech. When, at a gesture from the uniformed guard, he would roll his window down and thrust our passports through, he was closer to a heart seizure than to anything which could result in the naming of a destination or the purpose of a visit. My mother, in the meantime, would keep up an inane patter about anything and everything but the matter at hand.

The border safely crossed – and it is one of the least emphatically patrolled borders in the world – my father would drive for several miles, his eyes glued to the rear-view mirror. Only when we had put a safe distance between us and the frontier, would he begin to relax or explode into seemingly unconnected rage.

Returning to Canada was worse. An inveterate shopper, though she never herself carried any money, my mother would always have purchased more goods than it was altogether 'legal' to bring back into Canada. We're not talking here of major crime, but simply a little petty misdemeanour, an ordinary, everyday bit of getting away with it. Most products were cheaper in the United States. The journey home was always a nightmare. No sooner did we get into the car than the arguments started – an endless discussion of what would and wouldn't be declared on the Customs forms – my mother's new nightie, no; the pair of sheets, yes, and so it went on until the perspiration gathered on my father's brow and demanded silence, at which point my mother would usually burst into song.

As a child, I could never understand why these border-crossings were so excruciating, though for many years after I started to travel on my own, I would find myself edging into a nervousness akin to my father's when I approached a national frontier. Only recently did it come to me that the border dynamic between my parents was, in miniature, a reliving of their wartime experience. Its electric charge had little to do with the utterly innocuous passage between Canada and the US. For my parents, any official demand for documents, any confrontation with a uniformed being, sent them tumbling back into the emotional storm the Nazi occupation of Poland had produced. The double act they then involuntarily played out was a repetition of prior behaviour.

Faced by an official, my mother moved into flirtation mode. She could count on her beauty, her femininity, to achieve her ends. Long sideways glances punctuated by a flutter of eyelids and a slow smile would accompany an unconnected flow of seductive language designed by the very innocence of its patter to confuse. She never manifested any fear. Perhaps she didn't feel any. She thrived on the excitement of risk and performance. I suspect those expressionless Canadian and American border guards were relieved to see her go.

My father, on the other hand, was scared, just on the verge of uncontrollable panic. He masked it in a stiff lack of expression which matched the guards'. His words were terse, clipped responses which never made it to the length of a rounded sentence. Though he would meet the official's gaze full on with a stony impassivity, he never smiled. He gave the impression of having more important things on his mind, of being a man in a hurry. He was. He was in a hurry to get away.

My parents' different methods of dealing with such situations were entangled not only with their personalities but also with their appearance and gender. My father's hair and eyes were dark, his skin olive in hue, his nose a not insignificant protuberance. Under the kind of racial inspection which sought out such things, he looked like what he was – a Central European Jew. During the war, he had more or less effectively masked his features by sprouting a Hitler moustache. One stereotype helped to hide another. But there was one anatomical feature of the Jewish male's which couldn't join in the masquerade: that ultimately telling matter of a missing foreskin. As my father had good reason to know, appearances, the very sign of his masculine embodiment, marked him out as vulnerable. His body itself made him fearful. And from that the only escape was the death he was trying to avoid.

Trapped in this contradiction, it is hardly surprising that his hold on life always seemed more precarious than my mother's.

During my childhood, my father's image within the family didn't sparkle with legendary brightness. Unlike my mother and her intrepid missing brother, he never emerged as a hero of mythical stature. On the contrary. In my mother's repetition and progressive embellishment of wartime narratives, he was increasingly cast in what had by that historical moment, the fifties and early sixties, become the archetypal role of the Polish Jew. (Archetypes, like history, change with the times.) He was the timid, the retreating one – the man who would have chosen to die a ghetto martyr's death, were it not for my mother, the para-*shiksa*'s brazen courage. The role brought with it a taint of shame and, on my father's part, not a little subterranean anger.

'Your father's scared,' was one of my mother's constant refrains. 'He's always been scared.'

This accusation, half taunt, half casual aside, met only with a grumble and steely silence on my father's part. Because of its recurrence, we children always knew what my father was and had been frightened of. He had been frightened of Germans and the Gestapo and all men in uniform. He was now frightened of cops on motorbikes and border guards. He was frightened of tax inspectors and of filling out forms and indeed, of all the apparatus of State. He was also scared of lying and sometimes, it seemed, of speech and society itself. 'He's scared to pick up the phone,' my mother would mock.

Yet for all the uncontradicted reiteration of his fearfulness, while I was a girl my father never felt to me exactly afraid. He could plunge into freezing Canadian lakes and swim great distances, play a mean game of football. He gave off a kind of bullish stubbornness, a physical stolidity which always seemed on the verge of exploding into a show of strength. I had the impression that if necessary, he would bludgeon his way out of situations, punch the border guard, use his body against himself.

Once, this buried violence detonated in my direction. I still recall the scene vividly.

We were living in the third of our Canadian homes, a functional apartment in the Côtes des Neiges area of Montréal. From the flat roof of that block, my defiant brother repeatedly took potshots at pigeons with an air gun he had covertly acquired. I was about nine years old. My parents had just come back from work and I must have done something terribly wrong because my mother urged my father to punishment. She talked and talked and suddenly, he whipped his belt from his trousers. I raced into my room and flopped on the bed. The belt lashed my bottom, once, twice, three times. And then my mother tugged at him, told him to calm himself, it was enough – while I wept.

I no longer know what my crime then was. I only remember my sense of injustice and most acutely, the fierceness of my father's wordless rage. This seething anger was a more predominant mood than his fear – an emotion it sometimes collided with.

It seems to me now in the flickering wisdom that years bring, that there were good reasons for my father's anger. Though the fact never featured large in any of the ongoing narratives, he had after all lost the entirety of his immediate Polish family and most of his friends. A large portion of his self-respect had been battered out of him. The ferocity with which he beat his chest on the only Jewish holy day he scrupulously kept – Yom Kippur, the Day of Atonement – spoke more voluminously than any words he ever used. And yes, he was and had been afraid. State power – legitimate or illegitimate – could never in his judgement treat him as anything other than an undesirable alien. His fearfulness was the scar history had left him with. It was rooted in his lived experience. And that experience metamorphosed the very sign of his maleness into an object of terror.

My father Aron, the seventh of eight children and the second youngest boy, was born on October 4, 1913, to Estera and Reuben Borensztejn in the town of Pruszków, seventeen kilometres south-west of Warsaw. The town was a prosperous one, site of an important railway works, a large pencil factory and a well-known asylum. Its Jewish population in 1931 numbered only 1,288 out of a total of 23,647. The town had no synagogue of its own, though it did have a *beysme dresh*, a kind of meeting hall which doubled as a place of prayer and teaching. Almost a suburb, Pruszków was connected to Warsaw not only by train, but by trolley lines.

Story has it that great-grandfather Borensztejn, a railway engineer, came to Pruszków in the second half of the nineteenth century and was at least part, if not whole, owner of the railway works and engine servicing plant which became the town's largest employer. In his childhood, my father was fascinated by the site which stretched for almost the breadth of the town on the opposite side of the tracks. Chimney stacks breathed out columns of smoke, sparks flew, machinery crashed and boomed behind pyramids of coal.

Great-grandfather Borensztejn also acquired a substantial amount of property. For reasons unknown, perhaps to do with his death, or perhaps with the First World War, the railway works moved out of the family. During that war, his son, Reuben Borensztejn was taken prisoner by the Russians and accused of being a German spy. It was said – the accusation seems preposterous now – that he had radio communication equipment hidden in his beard. He was tried, his case fought by the Russian Zionist lawyer, Ginzberg, and won. None the less, Reuben returned home from his year in prison a broken man and retired to scholarly pursuits, leaving almost the entire running of the family textile firm to his wife, Estera. Though the family fortunes had by then declined somewhat, there was still enough wealth available for the two eldest sons, whom the war had washed up in Vienna, to be funded to go first to South America and eventually to the United States. It was the eldest, Abraham, who married one of the daughters of the Chief Rabbi of Vienna, made destitute by the First World War and happy enough to receive funds from a provincial entrepreneur.

Pruszków, with its proximity to Warsaw and relatively small Jewish population, was less of a conventional *shtetl* than my mother's Grodzisk. Apart from producing her brood of children, Estera Borensztejn was the dominant force in the family business, a role which was gradually passed on to her eldest daughter, Rosa, always according to my father a formidable businesswoman. In a photograph taken just after the First World War, Reuben wears Western dress and his beard is neatly trimmed along Edwardian lines. But religion still played a solid part in family life and in the charity distributed to poorer members of the Jewish community. For all his reputed post-war collapse and his increasing immersion in Talmudic study, Reuben was a man of stern patriarchal habits who ruled family life with an iron hand. Though my father's interests tended towards the intellectual rather than the entrepreneurial, he was taken out of school at the age of fourteen and put to work in the family textile firm whose premises occupied a substantial corner of the leafy church square. He was in awe of his authoritarian father – one of whose recounted habits was the intricate tying of shoelaces on the Sabbath to prevent his sons from stealing out to play football. They sneaked out barefoot instead.

The smallness of Pruszków's Jewish community meant both that there was more communication between Jews and Gentiles and that Jews were more easily recognised as such by the townspeople. My father's narrative of violent anti-Semitic incidents pre-dates the Second World War. Worried about inheritance, I once queried him about the slight indentation on his skull. 'A goy kicked me,' he said, and, ever terse, refused further elaboration. Brawls on the football field were numerous. There were more brawls after he joined the Zionist group of Bethar. Indeed, such bash-ups probably helped to consolidate his political choice of the militant Zionist grouping of which my mother's brother, Adek, was already a member.

And then there was the war, the time when all my father's smaller fears were welded into major terror.

When I pause to consider the differences between my parents, which in my childhood always seemed to coalesce under the two headings of blonde and dark, fearless and fearful, I can now see how they bore the stamp of an internalised Nazi ideology. Blondeness meant everything that was desirable, strong, powerful; darkness was weak, shameful, uncertain. Since she was blonde power itself, my mother's narrative about her life was never one of fear, either in the past or in the present.

But this all too common identification with the values of the aggressor, bore a particular inflection. There was no need to be afraid for she felt, insisted on feeling, that individuals were good – or certainly, at least, manipulable. And as far as their manipulability went, she was omnipotent. Abstractions like the State or the police or the nation or even politics and religion hardly existed for her. Only individuals who could return her gaze had reality. It was a useful form of denial and rendered her bold.

But what was denied seeped out and consolidated itself into an irrational, persecutory force. My mother believed – really believed – in the evil eye. With her emphasis on appearances, only an eye, of course, would do. We couldn't laugh or coax or tease her out of her small-town superstition. If anything went wrong, if we were ill or suffered some harm, it was because the evil eye had marked us out. As a child, I used to imagine a great dark pupil floating around in the ether, waiting to strike. If it fixed you with its envious gaze, you were done for. Worst of all, as my mother kept saying, all of this could happen without your seeing, while you were unaware. And it could happen at any time – at a bus stop or bakery or in the park. Only days later would you feel the evil eye's treacherous effect. My mother still believes in the evil eye and now that she is old and can no longer easily seduce, the power of the malevolent gaze has grown even greater. During the war, if she felt the evil eye flicker over her, she would flee the vicinity.

The evil eye, I suspect, is the name she chose to give to her sense that others were out to get her, to dent her great good luck, to see through her blondeness. By transposing her free-floating anxiety to a magical realm, she could maintain her illusion of power in the social world. Instead of my father's direct and named fears, she had one single superstitious one which she could balance out, almost in a Manichaean manner, with her blonde omnipotence. The existence of this magical repository for all her nameless fears, left her free to be fearless.

Odd Canadians

Like so many ambitious immigrants who want to secure their children's future, my parents worked hard. Six days a week, in blizzards or muggy heat, they travelled the miles to their various shops, often returning home well after dinner. Sunday was family day, which involved lunch in a restaurant and visits to or from friends. Some five years after we had arrived in Canada and by the time I was ten we had acquired a newly built house in the suburbs and eventually a daily maid. The maid, as history would have it, was German. 'The Germans are clean,' my mother announced, as if that explained everything.

Since my mother prided herself on not holding grudges and always insisted individuals were not the same as nations, I couldn't quite work out whether that meant she had altogether forgiven the Germans or in fact relished an opportunity for a dramatic up-ending of fate. This German, in any event, was emphatically a brunette and my mother rarely saw her face to face. Meanwhile my brother lorded it over her and I pretended not to notice her casually anti-Semitic grumbles. I don't think my father ever exchanged a word with her. When she was killed one icy night by a racing police car, he merely grunted. Maybe I imagined the glimmer of a smile on his lips.

Wartime stories continued to shadow this new home where everything else was proudly stamped 'Made in Canada'. Like doppelgängers, they would leap unexpectedly into the quiet suburban household and fill it with terrifying emotion. Increasingly, I baulked at their inappropriate presence. I told my parents enough was enough. They were Canadians now, even had the citizenship papers to prove it. My protests served little purpose. I couldn't understand then that repetition is also a form of forgetting.

Before I reached my teens, I don't recall my parents' or their friends' stories ever mentioning the word 'Holocaust'. The blanket use of the term to cover the entirety of the horrific experience of the Jews in the war only came with the late sixties. Its use emerged out of a tangled process of memorialisation, which inevitably contained not a little contemporary politics. Its tendency was – and still is – to merge all wartime experience into the one overwhelming experience of the killing camps. Grisly images of heaped skeletal bodies and emaciated prisoners in striped pyjamas took on an iconic value and mesmerised the imagination to the exclusion of all else.

The stories my parents and their friends told were both more particular and more diverse. They wore the jagged marks of individual memory which often won't fit neatly into the grand historical narrative. Once that second, collectively sanctioned narrative of an iconic Holocaust had achieved coherence and was paid tribute to – once they were all publicly recognised and memorialised as victims – their own storytelling began to fizzle out. By that time, I had left home.

But during puberty and my early teens, the very existence of these stories, the charged landscape of the past they inhabited as well as their endlessly repeated emotion, filled me with shame. I hated these stories. I couldn't bear them any more. None of them made any sense in our placid Montréal suburb where one house was so much like its neighbour that my father kept mistaking the street we lived on. Maybe all his wanderings had left no place on his inner map of the world for anything like a permanent home. The events of war had no reality in these peaceful, banal surroundings. Nor did the passion and drama which accompanied their telling.

I longed to bury the past and its traces. Above all, I longed to be as ordinary as all my suburban friends. They had nice, bland, bridge-playing, club-going parents. Parents who could speak English in full unaccented sentences. Parents who talked of mundane things, and not of concentration camps and ghettos and anti-Semitic laws and the dead and the missing. Their mothers baked cookies and cakes and provided scrumptious milkshakes after school and went to parents' meetings and charity functions. The children had swimming lessons instead of music lessons and they knew exactly where they had been born and what their names were. They had grandparents whom they went to see on Sundays and lists of uncles and aunts who delivered presents at appropriate times. Their fathers only read the Montréal papers and *Time* magazine and not on top of these a whole slew of newspapers in strange Hebrew script. Nor did they talk about Communism and Zionism, or indeed any other-ism.

I rarely brought any friends home and if I did, I made sure they left before my parents returned. Since Martha, the German maid, was somehow implicated in the whole wartime quagmire, it was best if she wasn't home either. All of which meant I spent a great deal of time in other people's houses. After all, you never knew when my mother might start in on one of her elaborate and embarrassing fictions. And my father had never mastered the art of small talk.

Despite all this, despite the fact that we spent so little time together, there was a closeness to the family bond. It had little to do with common interests or even common values. It was simply an intensity forged out of everything we had been through together and the fact that the family unit had no immediate extensions. Maybe all immigrants share that. Maybe, too, they share an unease about the emotionalism that kind of tight unit produces.

My first attempt to separate myself out from my family, which is what adolescent rebellion is mostly about, looked very much like a leap into conformity. No pierced lips and navel or blue hair for thirteen-year-old me. Under the influence of a friend's mother, a few of us set up a high-school-based B'nai Brith chapter. We held meetings with proper parliamentary procedure, named officers, had subcommittees and socials, baked cakes and sold jumble to raise money for Jewish charities, read through a heap of now forgotten literature, sang Hebrew folksongs and danced the Hora. This episode in my teenage life still has the power to embarrass me. Yet viewed

from the distance of the present, I can now see it as an attempt
to confront my mother's ambivalent relationship to her Jewishness. She might parade round as a *shiksa*, occlude her name
and origins, but her thirteen-year-old daughter would be
thoroughly honest and upfront. Well, almost. I could masquerade as a Canadian and be a public Jew.

The episode didn't last very long. Since my mother didn't
recognise rebellion, rebelling against her was always a difficult
business. As long as you returned her narcissistic need for
self-importance, she was prepared to accept anything. My leap
into conformity was as nothing to my brother's joining of the
then underground Communist Party. But the brown-paper-
wrapped book parcels topped with Soviet Union stamps which
arrived in the house didn't faze her either. And they soon stopped
as well. My mother's children, since they were extensions of
her, could do no wrong. The only form of rebellion she could
recognise was outright rejection or total separation. Sometimes
she even failed to recognise that.

My father was easier. With him at least you knew who the
enemies were.

Sometime in my thirteenth year, my parents made their first
return trip to Europe. They took me along. In 1959, the trans-
atlantic crossing still had the feel of a major adventure. London,
Paris, Amsterdam, Rome, Istanbul were names imbued with an
awesome glamour. My father was proud to be able to treat us.
We were all excited.

At some point in this giddy hip-hop between capitals, our
airline trajectory was changed and we had to board a Lufthansa

flight and make a stop-over in Frankfurt. My father's mood plummeted despite the even course of the plane. He sat stiffly in his window seat, his eyes lowered to his book. He refused to look up at the hostess, refused offers of food and drink. Not a word passed his lips for the length of the flight. Perhaps it was his visible rudeness which gave me the effrontery to engage in long and laughing conversation with the young German at my side, who happened to be even blonder than my mother.

When we were off the plane and safe on non-German soil, my father issued a terse command, 'You don't talk to Germans!'

The gauntlet had been thrown down. I raged, called him an old bigot, pointed out that the war was longer ago than my entire life, that one had to forgive and forget, and whatever other arguments my adolescent armoury held in store. The only retort I remember him making was the simple expletive, 'Never!' I still think that retort was at least in part responsible for my going off, once we returned to Montréal, to read Goethe and Fontane, as well as books about Hitler; my making friends with any Germans I could locate, and eventually taking courses in German. I became a whole reconciliation process in myself.

The last lap of our journey took us to Israel. Despite the intense summertime heat which turned beds into baths and an uphill stroll into a Himalayan challenge, my father was in ecstasy. He explored every new and ancient building, every terraced hill and freshly planted orchard, with the reverence of a pilgrim. He walked around kibbutzim with the light step of a youthful pioneer. He dusted off his prayerbook Hebrew and chatted to all and sundry. He felt, I guess, that he had come home to the imaginary homeland of his pre-war dreams.

One evening he said to me in a gleeful tone, 'Even the criminals here are Jewish.'

I worried over that remark. I don't think it arose from a sense that elsewhere he suffered from a great moral weight on his shoulders, a biblical injunction forcing him to be an exemplary man when he wasn't in Israel – though the embattled minority's burden of having always to prove oneself ethically superior is prevalent amongst Jews. I imagine it was more simply that he was happy to be in a place where what was for him a scarring difference between Jews and non-Jews didn't exist. He was at home in his body and his body was at home. No one here would point a gun or jeer if he lowered his trousers. When he dug his hands ceremonially into the hard Israeli soil and scooped away stones to make a space for the sapling marked as our family tree, he was joyous.

It took me a while to recognise that for him, Israel was both a memorial to the dead and the site of redemption. Its very existence signalled a triumph which metamorphosed horror and shame into useful martyrdom. The dead had not died in vain. All the dead of the Shoah had been retrospectively named citizens of Israel. Not that he believed the country was perfect. He was a pragmatic man. In the course of his life, he would bitterly complain about this or that feature of the country's development, criticise shifts in politics. But he was happy there. That first trip and subsequent ones marked the few occasions when I remember no rage in him.

My mother's case was altogether different. She was perfectly prepared to tolerate being in Israel, but she didn't really care for it. She manifested neither sentiment nor sentimentality about its existence as a Jewish state. It was all a little too rough and tumble for her. The pioneer spirit had never been her forte. Then, too, I suspect she had got so used to playing out her double act of being simultaneously Jewish and not Jewish that without its necessity, she felt lost. There was no place here for the survival skills she had so astutely honed that they had become all of her. Her act may have been a double one, but it was the only act she knew.

Israel remained a bone of contention between my parents. With a different wife, my father would certainly have settled there. But with a different wife, he might not have been alive to do so. So they stayed in Canada and occasionally argued over Israel. Sometimes these arguments soared to a triumphant pitch where my father would blurt out at her the irrefutable, 'Anti-Semite!', and my mother would shrug her trim shoulders and mutter her definitive riposte, 'Politics!'

One of the tangential results of all this was that my brother, after graduation from university, went to live in Israel and married what was then still a relatively mythical creature, a *Sabra*, a native-born Israeli – perhaps in part fulfilment of paternal, if not maternal, dreams. He stayed there for some three years before moving back to Montréal.

I, on the other hand, pursued what seemed at the time the more actively rebellious course. From the age of sixteen on, my love objects were never Jewish. I would covertly go out with and sometimes bring home Englishmen or Italians or Algerians or Québecois, whose overt anti-Semitism would secretly frighten me. I would watch my father turn stony in their presence and then lay down the always argued with and inevitably broken law as soon as they left. At night, I would hear his residual fury directed at my mother, who was, in traditional manner, meant to be in charge of her daughter's life. Bad enough, I was allowed the unspeakable liberty of going out with every Tom, Dick and Harry, but at least they could be Jewish. And my mother would calm him down and talk about phases and the vicissitudes of modern life and how intelligent I was and how people were people.

Marriage came on the eve of my twenty-first birthday. In part, I attribute the precocity of it to the fact that I needed to get away from the hothouse which was the family. A husband, then, seemed a useful and somehow more final bulwark than any extended period of study and career hopes, let alone the solitary flat I had inhabited for some years. The man in question was, of course, not Jewish. He was Italian: Catholic by origin and education. At the time, this caused not a little consternation.

'Jews aren't good enough for you,' my father fumed. 'You have to find yourself a lazy, uncircumcised artist.'

'He's circumcised,' I came straight back. Then to mollify his open-mouthed embarrassment at the fact that I had seen the difference, I added, 'Anyhow, he knows more about Jews than I do.'

Ever more persuasive, my mother tried a more reasonable tack. 'Mixed marriages ... they're so difficult. And money, a job ... You still have time to settle down.'

I shrugged rebellious shoulders and pointed out, matter-of-factly, that whatever they said, the choice was mine. This was Canada in the late 1960s after all, not 'Pipi-duvec' – the slighting joke name we all used for a make-believe *shtetl* lost in a doltish and archaic past.

In retrospect, given the family's buried internal dynamic, that underground war between shame and self-hatred, the choice of a Gentile was probably – all matters of love and romance aside – the inevitable course. One had to break free from those stories, even if their traces were so deeply imprinted they would mark any others one could live. Finding a name which was as distant as possible from all the permutations of my parents' was a manner of signalling the break.

The wedding took place in a reform synagogue. At that time civil marriages were prohibited in the province of Québec and finding anyone to marry us without conversion, one way or t'other, was a challenge in itself. A sign of this temple's singular liberalism was that the brides who preceded and followed me were so wondrously pregnant that honeymoons could only be spent in maternity wards. Though my parents and my new in-laws had both initially condemned the union and raged and worried over it, once it became fact, they resigned themselves and became fast friends. Gone were my mother's moans about what she would tell her circle. Gone my mother-in-law's tearful insistence – as if she had just put down her James Joyce – that her son at least tell her that he believed in God.

To their own surprise, the parents liked each other. Each side had their immigrants' stories to tell the other. The new audiences provided a refreshing change. Paradoxically, they remained firm friends even after my husband and I parted.

My rebellion, for all its surface noise, provoked no fundamental problems. Enmity was not part of my parents' vocabulary where their children were concerned. They might rebuke our transgressions. They might grumble. But eventually they accepted everything. They were simply happy if we were happy. They were simply happy that we were alive.

I guess I owe their equanimity to the war. Confrontation with death – too much of it, too brutal – has a way of making all other upheavals dwindle in importance. I suspect my main legacy from my parents is that they gave me a kind of deep fatalism. The worst has already happened and is bound to happen again. In the meantime, one is grateful. Grateful for small kindnesses and small generosities. Grateful for the gift of life. And free to be an optimist from day to day.

PART TWO

Excavations

Excavations

Like an ineffective sewage filtering plant run by opposing factions, my childhood left me with a sizeable residue of dark, uncertain matter, which could neither be instantly recycled nor thrown away. I was full of murky ambivalences about both Poles and Jews, full of rank prejudices too, which could be blown aside by the fresh air of good sense, but never quite obliterated.

When Lech Walesa emerged as the leader of Solidarity and the Catholic Church seemed, to so many of my friends, a force for liberation in Communist Poland, I couldn't altogether disguise my distrust of both – a distrust based on the paternal line that the Church in Poland is first and foremost anti-Semitic. Alternately, I could never quite get rid of my romantic sense that if the Jews were really to be Jews, they had to be in exile. Israel was all fine (or not fine) and well, but it was simply another country.

For a long time I kept a certain distance from matters which were distinctly Jewish or Polish. I was distrustful of the legacy I carried, wary of its admixture of truths, half-truths and lies all jumbled together in an emotional steam-bath which never washed one clean. It was easier to keep away, as it had been easier and perhaps necessary in my teens, to block out my parents' stories.

Oddly enough, I could cope with Germans and their history. Hitler was a monster and monsters who are universally acknowledged to be such are simpler to deal with. I read voraciously about Nazism, about the Weimar period out of which it had sprouted like an evil demon. I even wrote about it. Yet I stayed away from the intimate, unruly terrain of Poles and Jews. Maybe the familiar, the small differences in our midst, are trickier to contend with than the utterly unfamiliar. Civil wars are always bloodier, permeated with greater hate, than wars between distant opponents. We have to hammer out our guilt over the blinding wrongness of it in brutality.

'Poland is a cemetery!' my father would say, his eyes narrowing into fierce hatred. 'A desecrated cemetery. Mud and shit and bones and ash and scavenged graves. You don't play tourist in shit. You don't grow sentimental over shit.'

Have I mentioned that in his circle Aron was universally considered to be the gentlest of men?

Despite his very real breast-beating on the Day of Atonement, my father would never visit the cemetery that was Poland, nor entertain the possibility that any member of his family might do so. If the question came up in some social conversation, he would warn that any Jew who went risked being kept there by the Communists, risked being buried, dead or alive. Poland was a country where anti-Semites existed long after they had buried the Jews.

The wave of hysterical anti-Semitism which swept Poland in 1967 after the Six-Day War – in which the Soviet Union had supported the Arabs, and America, the Israelis – seemed to prove him right. Against the background of a struggle between opposing political factions, Jews, intellectuals and old-guard officials were interrogated about their racial origins, hounded out of jobs, arrested. Books and articles appeared alleging that Polish Jews had conspired with the Nazis in plotting Poland's ruin and were even now collaborating with the Germans. After slander, denunciation and what was effectively a purge, two-thirds of Poland's thirty thousand remaining Jews were forced into emigration.

Yet some of my father's friends travelled to Poland in the seventies. They brought back accounts of Eastern European poverty, of the forlornness or lack of memorials to the Jewish dead, of the eradication of a history which followed upon the slaughter of a people. My father would listen intently. At the mention of anything which meant bad news for the Poles, his face would light up. He always followed Polish and Eastern European news almost as avidly as news of Israel, though with opposite reactions. Grim news from the first met with an almost lascivious chuckle. It was as if he were cheering or booing hockey teams his loyalty had been assigned to from birth.

Though rationally I prided myself on being prejudice-free, and certainly tried hard to be so, unconsciously or unthinkingly I adopted my father's attitude. With modification, of

course. I had no interest in Poland at all. Not even any curiosity. Given that my youth was marked by curiosity about this,
that and everything, this was slightly bizarre. I was curious
about Britain and France and Italy and for a while, particularly,
Germany. I was curious about India and Afghanistan and
Tanzania. I was interested in the Soviet Union and
Czechoslovakia. Hungary, which family myth had it was filled
with wily, clever people, was a real draw. But not Poland.
Certainly not Poland, the country of my birth.

When, in my twenties, I mentioned this to a Polish aca-
demic colleague, who had exiled himself from the country in
1967, he reinforced my lack of interest. 'You're right,' he said.
'First the Germans killed off the best people. Then the
Communists finished off the few good ones they'd somehow
managed to leave behind.' I was too shy or too inhibited to ask
him if he meant the Jews. He wasn't one.

Now and again – since I was becoming that inherited and
very Polish-Jewish ideal I didn't know I had inherited, a 'cultivated' person – I would go and see a Polish theatre group of
radical experimentation, or read some startlingly fine poets,
admire Polish poster art or films. But it was only after my
father's death in 1981 that curiosity about Poland itself slowly
started to kindle. I made my first visit in 1988. I travelled in an
official capacity and with a colleague, Bill McAlister, who was
then Director of London's Institute of Contemporary Arts,
where I was Deputy Director. We were cultural emissaries,
guided and chaperoned and entertained. We saw theatrical pro-
ductions and performance work and films and film schools; we
visited galleries and art centres and museums, conferred with

artists and directors and filmmakers. The official capacity was a useful guise – particularly for myself. In no way was this to be a modish search for roots, though in a desultory manner I couldn't help but dip my toes into the muddy waters of early childhood. We took a couple of hours out from a crowded schedule to travel to the parental town of Pruszków where we snapped a few photos to show my mother. When we were in Łódź, the city of my birth, I found myself looking around the streets in the secret hope that some memory would surge up from the depths and produce a Proustian vertigo. Nothing. But then I hadn't bothered to find out the name of the street on which the family lived. Total adolescent rebellion against the past had slipped into a casual mid-life carelessness. I could take things Polish or leave them. Or so I thought.

What struck me forcibly during that trip was my own wary discomfort. I couldn't shed it. In part it was to do with the fact that we were always accompanied by an interpreter. Imagine a situation in which you understand some seventy per cent of what the person you are talking to is saying, but that person has no idea that you do. You're trapped in a fundamental duplicity. Caught in that falseness, you find yourself oddly vigilant – checking to see whether any asides have been made that don't warrant formal translation or what meanings the interpreter has decided to refocus, or whether someone has found you out because you've nodded or smiled before any translation has taken place.

My problem was compounded by the fact that – all formal reasons apart – I needed the interpreter. Polish and I have a mystifying relationship. I can understand it pretty well – far

better, say, than rapidly spoken Italian – yet I can barely bring
out a single word, whereas I can babble on in Italian or a
number of languages which I really understand far less well.
This inability to speak feels like a physical impediment – a
steep barricade which my stubborn, leaden tongue refuses to
scale no matter how much it is whipped by mind.

Since I have a soft spot for honesty, towards the end of some
of these extended conversations with Poles, I would bring out
the fact that I understood Polish. Because almost no one who
isn't, does, there would follow a quizzical glance, at which point
I would blurt out that in effect I had been born in Poland. The
glance would then turn into a blatant, assessing stare, followed
by a quick lowering of the lids and a tense moment of silence.
During all this, particularly if the person were my age or older,
I could hear a barrage of mute questions – about my Italian
name, my Mediterranean appearance, my age. And before the
solution to the puzzle could surface with its attendant and rapidly disguised embarrassment, I would stammer out, 'And yes,
I'm Jewish.'

The awkward silence would then prolong itself. One could
hear history tumbling through it with all its deaths, all its
mutual recriminations. Out of it an exonerating story would
unfold. Invariably, the story recounted how during the war that
person or a parent had saved or helped to save or simply helped
a Jew. All Poles, it seemed from my statistical extrapolation,
could be counted as brave friends of Jews. Given that in the
West Claude Lanzmann's film, *Shoah* had just brought radical
evidence to the contrary, given too what we all think we know
about the history of the Second World War, I was thrown into

something of a quandary. Either the people I met – who seemed decent in other respects – were simply liars when it came to the Jewish question. Or artists, writers, intellectuals, were different from all other Poles. Or *Shoah* and the received wisdom of the West that the Poles had been instrumental in ridding the world of Jews is not the whole truth. One monolithic truth, after all, rarely is. Child of the West, I, too, had my prejudices conceived in the crucible of family history and reinforced in the Cold War years which barricaded Poland in an Eastern bloc of anti-Semitism.

The uniformity of my current sample, I put down to good intentions. My hosts were as uncomfortable as I was when I raised this thorny matter of Jews. Poland, in the late eighties, was opening up to the West and taking on board its discourse of anti-racism, its clear message that anti-Semitism could not officially be tolerated. They were trying hard at least to appear to be on the right side. The effort needed to be applauded, reinforced.

When embedded prejudices are confronted in a situation where good manners are the norm, things inevitably grow prickly. One of our hosts, noting my discomfort, tried with diplomatic tact to ease matters by bringing to my attention all the fine work Poles were now doing in recovering the nation's memory of Jews. We were raced off to see a dramatised documentary about the Łódź Ghetto in which not a single Pole was portrayed, so that the ghetto existed in a nowhere, a floating island removed from context. We were also shown a feature about a turn-of-the-century *shtetl*, where all the Jews wore the hats and coats and, far more importantly, the superstitious attitudes of folklore. Our host considered this a wonderful film, proof of the fact that Poland was coming to terms with its Jews. I saw it as an exercise in mythography. Jews in Poland, it occurred to me, were fine as long as they could be framed in the exoticism of utter difference and had nothing to do with the complexity of recent history or common everyday encounters. Poles couldn't deal with Jews whose identity wasn't primarily bound up with a visible Jewishness. They couldn't deal with ordinary people who happened to have been born Jewish.

I was ordinary. I left Poland with no plans to return. It was as if my father's dicta had proved right. This was no country to visit. I wrote a glowing report about Poland's artistic efflorescence and put it all behind me. For good, I thought.

I hadn't counted on my mother's gradual and growing dotage to send me back.

She is sitting in front of the television. It is unclear whether she is watching the images flickering in front of her or some other scenario unfurling in her mind.

Suddenly she shouts, 'Quick. Quick come. There's my brother.' She points to a sportscaster on the screen. He is blond and handsome and all of thirty.

'That can't be your brother, Mum. This man's too young.'

'Get his name. Phone the television company. Quick.'

'It's not him.'

'Your brother would be eighty-five, Gran,' my son, Josh, interjects.

'Or maybe, eighty-three,' Katrina, his little sister, points out.

Hena looks from one to the other of us. Her eyes are vague. 'It's him,' she repeats stubbornly. Then, after a long moment's consideration, she adds, 'Or his son. Phone up, quick.'

Needless to say, we don't phone. This has happened before. It is to happen again and again. She sees her brother here, there and everywhere. He is a restless ghost, unburied. She doesn't speak to him as she does to her father. Her brother simply appears. As do, once again, her wartime stories. They make less and less sense now in their random interweaving, but since they provide a ready distraction from her growing and evident inability to deal with the real, we encourage her in the telling. It is better to hear her musing over the past than to engage in arguments over what day of the week it is, particularly since she stubbornly refuses our – and the calendar's – verdict.

My daughter Katrina and I reasonably decide that since she is so immersed in a misty past, it might be nice for her and useful for the children, if she could write it all down. We present her with a bound book, full of glossy white pages, together with a series of questions about what we want to know about her life. We want to know everything, Katrina explains, taking on the manner of a patient teacher talking to an obstreperous child: what her house looked like, her school, her friends, the war years. At least once a week, we ask her how the book is getting on. But her memories refuse the order of prose. Then too, writing, a solitary occupation, doesn't interest her: she wants the direct attention a listener brings.

The book lies untouched, its pages still blank.

*

As the months and years pass, I grow increasingly angry with my mother. I cannot bear the large cupboard which bulges with a mountain of plastic bags. I cannot bear her secret stash of soup tins, each enveloped in its own plastic bag and forgotten in her locked spare room. I cannot bear the coins wrapped in plastic inside a change purse wrapped in plastic inside a handbag, it, too, on occasion wrapped in plastic. If she must insulate her growing fragility, if she must hide her dying from herself, does she have to do it in plastic carrier bags!

I cannot bear her phoning me ten to twenty times a day and rambling on about the same nothing – the ingratitude and disrespect of my children whom she brought up so well until I ruined them. I cannot bear her constant and emphatic need of me, as if she could displace herself into my body and vampire-like dominate us both, all the while lamenting the way in which I have destroyed my life, which seems to me satisfactory except for her. I cannot bear her turning into an unreasonable, unattractive and selfish toddler, devoid of dignity or future. Nor can I bear her paranoia, her insistence that all and sundry steal from her, that only her incessant phone calls are unreturned by the doctor. Her recurrent moan that the world and everyone in it used to be so much better catapults me into frenzy.

'What!' I exclaim when I'm at my wits' end. 'The Nazis were better?' I am not, you'll remember, a particularly good or patient daughter.

She never deigns to answer that question. Perhaps it doesn't penetrate. She simply goes on, her babble unending. Her voice is her only remaining site of power and she inflicts it with zest.

It is not that I don't understand her loneliness. I know full well that youth was better for her than age. It is simply that I cannot bear the ever dwindling sphere of her life, its constriction to herself and her increasingly frail body. I cannot stand her stubborn refusal to see that the greatest part of her feelings are due to the condition of being old.

I smoke another dozen cigarettes in the hope that it won't happen to me. I dream of fleeing the country. Yet I am still here. It seems that I cannot be as bad a daughter as I wish. I remain her only daily link to the world outside her body.

She sits in her kitchen in front of her magnifying mirror. 'We're late, Mum,' I say for the tenth time. I am taking her out for lunch and we are indeed very late.

'I've got these black spots on my face,' she mumbles. She rubs more and more cream into her skin. 'I can't go out with these black spots. My whole face is black.'

'There are no spots on your face, black or red or any other,' I say. I have said this before. I have said it over and over for at least a year. I have talked to the doctor about the non-existent black spots.

'The doctor gave me this cream,' she says and continues her rubbing.

'The cream is a cleanser,' I repeat. 'Aqueous cream. You wash with it.'

She won't budge from her mirror. She sits there gazing at herself and rubbing at the invisible spots.

Lady Macbeth of Highgate. Or perhaps Narcissus, that minor deity, but God to those who live by appearances.

*

It is in part for my own sanity, that I decide to explore her past.
I need to undo her diminishment. I don't want this image of
her to usurp all others. So I set out to elicit her stories from her
in a systematic way, pen at the ready. Her memories, of course,
elude system.

The familiar biological irony of all this doesn't escape me.
This is the ultimate generation game. All my friends are playing it. We are suddenly interested in our parents' pasts which
we feel are linked with our own buried ones. Children of Freud
and his mismarriage to the rebellious sixties which put youth,
only youth, on a pedestal, we root around, often too late, in the
family romance and sometimes excavate dark secrets. We are
hungry for knowledge. If it doesn't, at its best, bring mutual
understanding or forgiveness, or, at its worst, an excuse for personal failure, at least it may bring a kind of peace. Perhaps even
a childhood talisman to inure us against old age.

In my case, I am all too aware that my parents' past is a narrative in a foreign and forgotten language. During the brief
span of time when their memories were still relatively fresh and
I was capable of grasping some of their resonance – my teenage
years – I wanted nothing to do with them. When I had put an
ocean between us and grown distant enough to be able to allow
myself a genuine interest, the memories had already congealed
into a series of tableaux. Staged by my mother, these tableaux
took on brighter and brighter colours, painted over the horrors
of the war from which they had emerged. Increasingly, she
denied what she didn't want to know or chose to forget. Only
the grim set of my father's face, the occasional interjection of
a shattering comment, punctured her gilded balloon and

forced it to land amongst the shattered lives of the ghetto or the camps. But my father didn't particularly want to remember either. He kept his silence. Six years of single days which linked my mother's set pieces gradually disappeared into the scarred receptacle which is an identity.

Memory is always a montage of disparate fragments. In order to put these fragments into some kind of sequence, I need to set her memories now side by side with the fuller versions I remember from childhood and my own youth. There are also my brother's memories and those of the few remaining friends. I grill them all. I also watch, over and over again, the so-called Survivor Interview my mother gave to a 'Living Testimony' research team at McGill University in Montréal in 1991.

Hena stares out at me from the screen. Her honey-coloured hair is fluffed up, her face almost free of wrinkles. She looks at least twenty years younger than her seventy-six. And she is visibly thrilled to be in front of the camera. People want to listen to her without interrupting. She smiles and smiles, lowering her eyes for dramatic emphasis as she weaves her web of story. Her tone is excited. She is once again a heroine of our times, a bold young woman who outwitted dreaded foes. And in her heroism, she is generous. There are good people everywhere, good Germans and brave Poles. Sometimes, when she talks of her father or brother or son, the tears rush to her eyes. She brushes them away quickly and returns to her narrative. Oddly, my father is almost written out of the story. I don't mind her forgetting his grimmer war. Forgetting is as necessary as remembering. I am happy to see her like this. It makes me forget the way she is now.

Yet when I look at my transcript of the video, I am startled at how fragmentary her narrative is. Each fragment makes sense on its own, but nothing coheres – as if the only point of cohesion were her own speaking body. Without it, dislocation rules. There is an occasional winter or spring, but there are no dates. Everything floats in a limbo crowded with detail which evades sense. The burning of the Warsaw Ghetto is an aside – a smoke-filled view from a new flat. My mother's story is devoid of history.

I rush to the history books. I read and read. History makes sense of memory. It gives one a grid for individual experience. It provides a panorama of troop movements and official decrees. It offers up statistics and above all pattern. History, after all, is written with hindsight. Ends are already known. It comes to me with the force of a paternal thump on the shoulder – the kind that sent me plunging into icy waters – that while my parents lived the war, it was a frenzied rush of days and nights, any of which might have brought the war to an end, or their own lives. Confusion ruled. The unstructured moments of my mother's memory echo that confusion.

None the less, I still need to rid myself of some of my own. My parents' wartime story refuses to ground itself. I cannot smell its rubble or bombs or fear. I cannot see its hostile faces. London is simply too far away, geographically and emotionally. When I first came to Britain and heard people talking about the war, I thought I had travelled to an enchanted planet somewhere between Venus and Mars. The war here was a series of heady dances, attractive American soldiers, outlandish school-boy pranks in the desert, and stammering men in specs cracking Enigma codes. Bombs were beautiful flares in the night sky from which people ran into shelters to exchange jokes and hot tea. Jewishness was certainly not an issue. There was never a Jew in sight.

No. I finally realise that if I am going to make any sense of my parents' war and my sudden interest in it, I am going to have to visit the sites of memory. I will have to travel to Poland.

Perhaps the journey is simply a devious way of putting some distance between myself and the Lady Macbeth of Highgate.

On Site

The airport at Warsaw is new and bright and shiny. The immigration official moves her lips into what could almost be a smile and says 'Dziękuję.' Thank you. There is no scowl above the uniform at Customs control. A formal welcome to Poland beams from every freshly dusted and painted corner and only asks in return that we welcome Poland into the community of Europe. Everything has changed since my last arrival here in 1988. Poland is now keen to board up the spectre of Communism in some inviolable dungeon and to bury within it all its former associations with the Soviet Union – as keen as it once was to forget the sorry war years. Like shifting tectonic plates, the nation's remembering and forgetting heave and grind against each other to the rhythms of political change. History is there to be written over. And over.

I am not travelling alone. Out of a need for ballast, I have invited my old friend from New York, Monica Holmes, to come with me. I don't want to be blown towards the choppy waters of sentimentality, always a prey to those travelling alone; or worse in my case, towards a pleasant sea of distractions.

(Who needs the Holocaust, when there are wonderful oils to look at!) Monica is not only a formidable and determined traveller: she also speaks the language, which makes using the telephone a distinct possibility. Polish is a language so crowded with multi-clustered consonants, five-syllable words, variations on the sh/sz, not to mention the cz/dzy/krz/prz/trz sounds, scores of diminutives, masculines and feminines which demand intricate agreement, that reading the guide to telephone use for someone who has only ever heard the language takes more concentration than a page of *The Critique of Pure Reason*.

Then, too, Monica and I share an overlapping history. We were both born in Poland, she before the war, I after. Her father, Dr Gustav Bychowski, was Warsaw's first psychoanalyst. After taking his medical degree at the University of Zurich, he worked with Bleuler and then Freud, before returning to Warsaw to set up in private practice. Nineteen twenty-eight saw the publication of his *Handbook of Psychoanalysis*, the first work in the field to appear in Poland. In 1935, he was named Professor at the University of Warsaw medical school. He also worked closely with Janusz Korczak, the extraordinary doctor and humanitarian thinker, who ran a Jewish orphanage in Warsaw until he and all his remaining children were transported to Treblinka.

Gustav Bychowski and his family – his second wife, step-daughter, and Monica, then two – left Warsaw literally on the eve of war and drove east in a Hillman, too small to have been commandeered for the war effort. When the Hillman ran out of petrol, it was abandoned and replaced with a series of horse-drawn carts which eventually brought them to Wilno or

Vilnius, then in Poland, now in Lithuania. From here, they succeeded, first in retrieving their sixteen-year-old son whom the war had trapped in a Scout camp and then in getting to Sweden where they spent some eighteen months waiting for a US visa arranged by the American Psychoanalytic Association. By the time it arrived, travelling westwards proved impossible and the journey to the US had to be made by train through the freezing expanse of the Soviet Union, then to Japan in a clapped-out boat which sank on its next voyage, and finally to San Francisco. Their travels were plagued by incident and illness, but the only part Monica remembers clearly is the time spent on the Trans-Siberian Express. She had whooping cough and everyone, particularly the friend who was travelling with them under false papers, feared she would draw attention to them and have them chucked out into an ice-bound *terra incognita*. To keep her quiet and to prevent her from using his real name, as she threatened to do, the family friend was forced to tell her Gogol's story, *The Nose*, over and over again.

Monica and I both regret not paying enough attention to our childhood stories of war and emigration. We are both aware that it was necessary not to. The diffuse anxiety and fear, the charged family atmosphere of those times, is precisely what we needed to shed in order to become functioning New-World beings. Our older siblings had a far harder time of it. They couldn't quite so readily create a viable amnesia – or cast off that accent which is a visible trace of foreignness. None of which lessens the regret, particularly now when our children would like to know. So total was Monica's rejection of those years and the narratives which circulated about them, that she had to ask her husband whether her family had landed at Ellis Island. Which of course, they hadn't. She knew and yet she didn't know – in that fuzziness peculiar to childhoods scored by tragedy – that they had arrived in San Francisco, that her elder brother had stayed on there to study at Stanford, that after a semester during which he learned English well enough to write for the *New York Times*, he travelled to England, enlisted in the Polish squadron of the RAF, and was shot down twice – the second time, just before the war's end, fatally.

So here are the two of us in Warsaw trying to mend or perhaps simply understand something of our fractured relationship to Poland and the past.

We are met at the airport by Andrzej Latko and his son, Robert. Andrzej is the one remaining contact of my mother's in Poland, the single living tie to history. His father, Stanislaw, was my parents' landlord during the Warsaw Uprising, when Andrzej was a boy of nine. The families made contact again after the war and kept in touch even after Stanislaw's death in 1957. I still remember my parents shipping parcels laden with clothes and food from Canada to Poland, during the long years of scarcity.

Andrzej now embraces both Monica and myself and proffers two bouquets of delicate yellow roses in welcome. We are touched by the Old-World gesture and by the fact that he has taken the trouble to come and meet us. He is a handsome man, white-haired and hale. An economist for various electrical plants during the Communist years, he is now semi-retired, a part-time consultant. In the course of our visit, as we ply him with questions about the great change in Poland's political destiny, his twinkling blue eyes crinkle with wry irony. His mood is both genial and philosophic. Yes, he says, things are better. There is more traffic and everything is available. There are more and better restaurants and some people can afford to go to them. People are permitted to travel freely, but unfortunately not for free. Yes, depending on who's doing the counting and where, things are better for about seventy per cent of the population.

'Less than fifty', his son, Robert, mumbles. Robert, a computer systems troubleshooter for a bank, is a boyish thirty-seven, fair and pink-cheeked and a little stiff with seriousness. He is uncertain about these visitors from foreign lands. He has never travelled abroad. He is particularly uncertain about Monica who stands in for all his suspicions about America which equals rampant, uncaring capitalism, the excesses of consumerism, and an imperialist pop culture which threatens all local culture. It also equals escalating street crime and youth gangs and freedom bordering on anarchy, which means no security, physical or financial. Not that he says any of this overtly, but it is evident in his leading questions and rigid gestures. Nor is it that he has any time for Communism, that hoary imported bogey from the East which spread a leaden stench over the country he loves. It is more simply that we all continue to carry some of the baggage we are brought up with and Robert was brought up with suspicions about America and its seductive exports. If asked, he would say he has no interest in politics.

Few Poles do, his father glosses for us with one of his more gnomic twinkles. No one cares about politics except the politicians, who have something immediate to gain from it.

I am reminded that years of one-party rule are hardly designed to generate abiding political interest. And now that the one overriding desire, independence from Big Brother to the East, has been achieved, politics is for the professionals. Ordinary Poles get on with the hard enough business of day-to-day life, and scarcely even bother to vote. The turn-out for the last general election was under fifty per cent.

We pile into a small white Polski sedan, the local Fiat, and drive through night-time Warsaw. The car has all the internal furnishings I remember from my Québecois childhood when cars were still treated as precious possessions to be protected from time: furry covers on seats and headrests, an array of stickers and dangling creatures and deodorants. Robert prefers us not to smoke. This new and growing prohibition on smoking, which we encounter in trains and stations and parts of restaurants throughout our visit, is a certain sign of preparation for entry into the European Community, the first and healthy world of affluence. When I was last in Poland in 1988 the same large cross which now exes out cigarettes, exed out cameras. Photography was prohibited. My colleague, Bill McAlister, was marched off to an iron-barred cell for daring to take a picture in a railway station and it required a lot of talk and showing of passports and threats of ambassadorial interference to extricate him. The photo was of a poster, pinned on the railings of the Lublin station and announcing a community dancing school. He took it because this was one of the few posters we saw anywhere.

In 1997, the world of Soviet-style secrecy and fear of the stolen image is gone. In its stead there is the beginning of a Western anxiety about the body. Meanwhile posters and billboards with their beautiful, young dream bodies have sprouted everywhere. They recline on the sides of the road as we drive, lean out of the walls of buildings in the brightly illuminated streets of the city centre. Despite my mixed feelings about advertising, subliminally I used to crave such posters and hoardings when I travelled in the East in the days before the Berlin Wall came down. I couldn't understand why everything looked so grey and dank and dull. I used to joke that the one truly useful artistic exchange we could offer the East lay in megagallons of paint and teams of house decorators. But my eyes, conditioned in the West, also missed the splashes of colour publicity images provide. Now they are here in Warsaw and a proportion of the buildings behind them wear bright new coats. The city feels far more welcoming than I remember it.

We arrive at our hotel, the Europejski, a grand nineteenth-century edifice overlooking the Tomb of the Unknown Soldier. The hotel was reconstructed after the Second World War and it still has the feel of an old Central European establishment, despite the wave towards seventies conference modernism of its interior. I perch at the edge of a black leather sofa, capacious enough for several Boris Yeltsins, and sip the coffee everyone else has refused. It takes me a few minutes to realise that drinks in the lobby bar are Western in their prices. As our nominal hosts, Andrzej and Robert refuse our protests and insist on treating us, but four drinks would mean an exorbitant expenditure. So I sip the strong, acrid coffee alone and exclaim a guilty '*Bardzo Dobrze*', very good, in response to Andrzej's query about its quality. Guilt at Andrzej's generosity and kindness hovers over me throughout our stay in the country. The textured ironies of a Jew feeling guilty in Poland only strike me when I get home.

Through Monica, who acts as my interpreter, I explain to Andrzej the purpose of my visit. He studies me closely for a moment, and then despite the growing lateness of the hour plunges right in and tells me how he remembers meeting my mother in the spring of '43. He was playing outside the house in Sadyba on the outskirts of Warsaw when she arrived, a pretty blonde, well-dressed, softly-spoken, cheerful. She asked for his father who was out at work, so she wandered around until his return. The next day she and my brother moved into the two back rooms of their flat. Andrzej, who was motherless, liked having them there. They would often eat together, play.

'And my father?' I ask.

'Kazik? At first he only came on weekends. He worked in a chemical factory on the other side of Warsaw. When he came, he liked a drink and to socialise. He would sit with my father and sometimes a neighbour from across the street and drink and chat. He taught me to swim.' Andrzej laughs, his face crinkling with pleasure.

'Swim?' I echo. I have a sudden image of my father hurling me into a Canadian lake and simultaneously a visceral tug which I can only describe as the tug of history. I sink into the black leather of the sofa. My voice seems to squeak in imitation of its sound. 'He taught you to swim in the middle of the war?'

Andrzej shrugs. 'On some days there was more war than on

others. Kazik liked swimming. And he taught me. He threw me in. I'll show you where. Tomorrow or the next day.'

I nod. 'And your mother, Andrzej, she was Jewish?'

There is a sudden silence round the low table, as thick as its wood. Robert, I notice, is looking intently at his father.

'No,' Andrzej shakes his head.

'I must have misunderstood.' I scramble through an apology. 'My mother led me to believe . . . '

'No, no,' Andrzej's denial is vigorous. 'She was baptised,' he adds and looks towards his son as he rushes on. 'I really hardly remember her at all. She had tuberculosis and was already very ill when my father came back from the Front. It was a terrible winter, that winter of '39–'40, the worst in memory. My father sent her off to a sanatorium in Otvosk. She died there of pneumonia in 1940. There is no grave. At that point of the war, there were only mass burials.'

'I'm sorry,' I hear myself saying inanely.

My first few hours in Poland and already stories refuse to tally. In my family, there is certainty that Andrzej's mother was Jewish. In the ordinary run of affairs it would hardly matter. During the war it mattered. As I steal a glance at Robert's face, I have a lingering sense that maybe here it still does.

Climbing the circular staircase to my room, I am left wondering whether Stanislaw Latko simply found it more expedient, given the course of Poland's wartime and post-war history, not to taint his son, Andrzej, with his wife's ambiguous origins.

The next morning we breakfast in a long thin rectangle of a restaurant amidst a babble of tongues – Korean, Dutch,

German, French, Polish. Only Russian is conspicuous by its absence. The spread is sumptuous – platters of cheese and meat and herring, vast bowls of fruit and an assortment of bread and sweet buns. I gorge myself on fern-scented blueberries and thick, moist slabs of yeasty bread. I have deep childhood memories of bread, olfactory memories. Bakeries draw me in by the nose. A particular whiff and like Alice, I tumble through the looking glass and become very small. With the smell comes a mixture of desire and excitement and pleasure. Recently, in one of her meanderings, my mother gave me a clue to the special place bread holds in my life – a specialness I have always associated with an early memory of Poland. There was a bakery two doors down from our apartment in Łódź. Its smells lingered in the street, wafted round us every time we passed. Once when I was sent there on my own, the baker apparently gave me a wad of money he owed my father along with our bread and told me to rush straight up with it. Framed in a non-existent snapshot, I can see this other person which is my small self toddling home on plump legs. I am puffed up with responsibility, the double pleasure of self-importance and warm, scented bread.

Opposite the hotel is a military barracks. Four soldiers in thick grey-brown uniform march out of its doors towards the vast paved square which houses the Tomb of the Unknown Soldier. We follow in their trail. The day is cold and dank, the sky a shuttered grey canopy. The visible decay of the National Theatre, the brutal glass and concrete of the Intercontinental Hotel which flank the square render the city less welcoming than the twinkling lights and shadows of the previous evening.

We watch the stiff-legged dance of the changing of the guard and then, reminding ourselves that we are not simply here as tourists, we carry on into the grounds of the Saxon Park. Monica used to be wheeled here as a toddler by her nanny. The words Ogród Saski carry a resonance of pleasure for her. And the park is pretty. Chestnuts large enough to pre-date wartime bombs spread their autumn foliage above the chattering ducks of the lake. Neatly planted beds of marigold and jungle red gladioli vie with the ashen light.

The cold makes us walk quickly. Our beacon is a tower to the north-east which bears the word Sony at its crest. Huddled at the base of the giant block is the narrow Ulica Tłomackie. On it stands the Jewish Historical Institute, an imposing structure initially designed in the late twenties by the architect Edward Eber as a principal Judaic library. In 1943, when the Germans destroyed the great Warsaw synagogue, they also set fire to the library. In 1947 it was rebuilt to house the newly created Institute and its invaluable wartime archive, as well as a library and museum. Now, a sign announces that the museum is closed for reconstruction. Yet the door swings open. We have not come in vain.

Inside, the low light of a single bulb illuminates a crumbling cavernous space with rolled carpets and draped furniture. It takes a moment to make out a heavy double-winged staircase, a small bookshop tucked to its left. From the right, a voice beckons and we turn to see a makeshift reception desk. We explain to the woman who sits behind it that we are bound for the archives and have an appointment with Peter Rytke the archivist who works under Director Yale Reisner, with whom I have been in communication.

Most of the archives here were gathered together in the forties and fifties. There are extensive pre-war records of the ancient Jewish communities of Wroclaw and Krakow, amongst others. There are records charting the activities of various post-war committees. Sixty per cent of the archive, however, is devoted to the history of the Holocaust and the wartime ghettos. It is here that the extraordinary 'Underground Archive of the Warsaw Ghetto' – a mass observation project set up by Dr Emmanuel Ringelblum at the start of the war whose end he didn't live to see – was put together from the charred and soiled papers found amidst the rubble of the ghetto. It is here, too, that one can find records of the Jewish Councils, the Judenrat, and of the Ghetto Uprising.

We make our way up two steep floors laden with dusty relics of furniture and giant stone sculptures. On the third landing a door swings open and a young man walks through it. He is blond, blue-eyed, chunky, with the flat face and open features I have always associated with Polishness. Peter Rytke manages to be at once perfectly courteous and altogether perfunctory. As he points us towards a small table topped by a row of blue-bound alphabeticised tomes, he manifests no particular interest in us, nor our quest for recorded traces of our families. We are a distraction from his principal task which is that of archiving Poland's Jewish past. The living are patently an interruption.

The blue-bound tomes contain rows upon rows of names collected immediately after the war by the Centralny Komitet Zydow Polskich – the Central Committee of Jews in Poland. Each name denotes a survivor who has come to this agency in Warsaw – from elsewhere in Poland or returned from Russia or

Romania or Israel or the United States – in search of missing relatives or friends. In all there are some 200,000 names registered. Each name is linked to an index card which provides additional information about the individual. These lists are the first port of call for anyone searching out Polish Holocaust survivors.

Like a child learning to read, I work my way slowly through the list of B's, my index finger marking the route along the thin sheets of poorly typed and mimeographed paper. When I come across a Borensztejn, Aron, a shiver goes through me. With it comes the realisation that I had assumed this foray into archives was a ritual I felt I should undertake, but one attended by the certainty that no tangible discovery would be made. Now that my father's name perversely leaps out at me, I am at a loss. Despite my middle age, the child inside me, like all omnipotent infants, has had difficulty in believing that my parents really did lead a life which pre-dated me – a life outside of story and family myth. But here in front of me, on this rickety table in an old Warsaw building, is the historical proof. I stare at it, unable to make a sound, then quickly take down a second volume of this peculiar register and flick through the L's. Amongst the Lipszycs there is a Sura, an alternative Yiddish spelling for my grandmother, Sara.

Peter Rytke brings me the numbered information cards which pertain to the two names. My father's name elicits two cards, which, Peter Rytke explains, could mean that he came to the registry twice, and indeed, although the yellowing cards bear no precise dates to indicate when exactly they were filled out, each one gives a different address: the first in the town of

Pruszków is Kraszewskiego 13/8; the second in Łódź is Legionów 55, which is also the address on my grandmother's card, so the two names really do refer to my family and not others with the same names. I have been told that my grandmother lived with my parents when they moved from Pruszków to Łódź where I was born. From the cards, I also learn the names of maternal great-grandparents. Bits of family history begin to take on a specificity they never before possessed as narrative and recorded fact coalesce. The addresses have a particular import. They give me a tingle of investigator's triumph, the kind I imagine Maigret must have experienced when a case began to come together. I can now visit not only my parents' but my own first home.

The discrepancies on the yellowing cards – one of them, presumably because of the lack of paper, overprinted on the back of a German document – fascinate me. On each of them, my father gives a different date of birth: what I imagine is the first states 1911; the second, 1919. I had always been told he was born in 1913. I imagine the chaos of Warsaw in 1945 and I tell myself that dates of birth must have seemed infinitely negligible. All that mattered was being alive. Or dead. Greater exactitude than that is for historians.

On one of the cards, my father gives an alternative name: Zabłocki. It is one of his wartime aliases. Yet here it is post-war and he is still using it. Perhaps it is Zabłocki who had one of these alternative birth dates. Aliases, as I should know but am still to learn, are not altogether easy to shed.

Of my missing uncle, the primary object of my search, there is no trace. I had hardly expected, so many years on, to find a trail where my parents had failed. Yet new materials do turn up and are now far better archived than before, here in Warsaw. Prior to my departure for Poland, for good measure, I contacted the International Red Cross tracing service as well as the Yad Vashem archive in Israel. But I can't help feeling that some sighting of Adek here in Warsaw would be a particular boon.

Peter Rytke brings out more search materials – a registry of bank accounts held in Poland's national bank before the war, a 1938 Warsaw telephone directory. In the first I find my paternal grandmother listed. In the second, a name which must be my missing uncle's: he appears as part of a firm called 'Gdynia' together with two partners, one of whom was to become his father-in-law. These mundane fragments of recorded fact make me grateful to our archivist.

Surprisingly, his utter lack of interest has gradually been replaced by something like excitement. The turning point comes when Monica finds her father's number in the telephone directory, the 'Dr' prominent in front of it, together with a list of most of her family, publishers and booksellers, a veritable cultural aristocracy. Perhaps our archivist is pleased to have a rare visit from an uncommon Jew, one whose origins are outside the *shtetl*. Whatever the reasons, he is suddenly busy with us, ringing the university records office, dropping a few intriguing hints about himself – the fact that his mother is a rabbi's daughter, the fact that he is working on material for the Holocaust exhibition at London's Imperial War Museum. While he rushes off to make phone calls and photocopies, we chat to another couple who have climbed the steep staircase to this windowless landing. Israelis, they are originally from

Warsaw. Small children when war broke out, both made their
way through Russia, Bombay, Iran, and eventually at the age
of ten landed in Haifa. Yet they only met years later and when
they did, promptly married, their kinship already formed
through the shared experience of war and deportation.

Peter Rytke ushers us through a door into the archive's inner
sanctum, a large airy space flanked by computers which shout
their modernity to ceiling-high columns of cardboard boxes –
a veritable Himalaya of files in the centre of the room. A computer produces a print-out on Grodzisk for me. It cannot do
the same for Pruszków, since that letter has not yet been
reached on the data-base program which provides information
on Poland's towns and cities, their Jewish population, their syn-
agogues and cemeteries, the dates that ghettos opened and
closed down so that their remaining populations could be
shipped to the principal deportation site: Warsaw.

We are shown two thick scrapbooks of photographs of children. There are smiling little girls with party bows in their hair,
arranged in just the way my mother used to do mine. There are
children playing in the street, others with wide sombre eyes
staring into the camera, mostly girls again. These are photographs of Jewish children who were placed for safety during the
war in Christian orphanages or with adoptive parents. After
the war, Peter Rytke tells us with grim disapproval, Jewish
agency workers in the grip of anti-Polish sentiment ripped
these children, many of whom were too young to know they
were Jewish, from the care of often loving adoptive parents and
packed them off to kibbutzim in Israel without a thought for
their emotional welfare. Only occasionally were these children

eventually matched with missing parents or relatives. The
bureaucracy of vengeance had its own ideological heartlessness.

As if we have responded in the right way to these haunting
images, Peter Rytke rewards us each with a poster-size photo-
copy of the old Warsaw synagogue. I gaze out of the window,
wish for a prohibited cigarette and suddenly lose my bearings.
In front of me stands an elegant structure of moulded grey
stone which looks uncannily like the poster in my hand. But
it cannot be. The old synagogue was blown up on May 16, 1943
on Jürgen Stroop's orders as a sign of the Nazis' final victory
over the Warsaw Ghetto Jews who had dared to resist. I stare
at the building and see a dark-haired woman move closer to the
window to look back at me. It takes me a long moment to
recognise my reflected image. The mirrored facade of the Sony
Tower encloses and replicates the Jewish Historical Institute
and has framed me in postmodern parody. I am both inside the
old and inside the new looking back at myself. I have an eerie
sense that in this search to make my mother's memories real,
to return her past to both of us, I may be entering the ultimate
hall of mirrors.

The next morning Monica and I make our way towards the
huge pseudo-gothic excrescence which is Warsaw's towering
cultural centre, a building loved solely because it is the only
place in the city from which it can't be seen. Two sides of the
square round the centre – distressingly bare in 1988 – have
now been given over to a sprawling market, an emporium of
open-air boutiques where any manner of attire can be purchased, though we witness few purchases being made. Our

first destination is the suburban-line station, a gaping underground site beneath the market square. The family towns of Pruszków and Grodzisk are both on the Zyrardow line, a clattering suburban ride on outdated stock westward out of Warsaw. We both feel that these carriages with their low hard seats and encrustations of grime could well be the same ones my parents commuted in.

As the train creaks and groans through two outer Warsaw stops, we see graffiti warring with history. Like bright, raucous flowers, the messages spill out of crumbling concrete of Soviet make. Fuck the norm, blares one. Love, shouts another. English seems to be the preferred language both of freedom and urban squalor. We chug past allotments, their dahlias and chrysanthemums blazing orange and red and yellow between sheds topped with corrugated iron. We move into leafy countryside. Near Plastów, there are pretty wooden dashas and ornate rural retreats. Past the looming grey bulk of Pruszków station, where we will stop on our way back, the chestnuts are nipped by autumn rust. Spacious birch forests sparkle in a whiteness of bark. Orchards are heavy with plum and apple. Dappled cows graze alone or in twos in small plots. The landscape is innocent.

An old woman, heaped stringbags of groceries on either arm, walks a straight dirt path beside the track. Children cycle past her and past us, past simple houses with deep sloping roofs. A horse with a U for a back stands in the midst of a field, a kerchiefed kneeling woman and an ancient wooden cart at its side. Hand-made hay ricks dot the horizon. There is a timelessness to it all which lulls the senses. Poland's traditional and impoverished peasantry still forms a substantial part of its population. Nearly half the land is given over to agriculture. Indeed, that is one of the problems confronting the country's entry into the European Union. I find myself wondering in what ways this peaceful, unchanging vista might have been different during the war. Did that old man who now sits at a crossroads, his heaped potatoes spread on the verge beside him, gather his wares and run into the shrubbery as an armoured car passed? Did this road resonate with the trooping of boots and the sound of fire? And that dilapidated freight train, perched on a neighbouring track, did it once serve the Nazis' Final Solution? Or the bleak conductor, rude in his demand for tickets, would he once have asked for far more? A lice pass, perhaps – or worse, an identity card? The slow chugging of this old train in this older countryside wakens the ghosts.

They flit about us as we disembark at Grodzisk. The pretty, freshly painted station with its colonnaded porch and frilled turret is reminiscent of an Austrian spa town. But beyond it, there is no nineteenth-century spa, only a sixties renovated pedestrian zone with even newer shops beneath iron-work balconies and a few sparsely peopled cafés.

I hide my disappointment. Had I in nostalgic unreason really expected a Chagall-scape, an exotic site of crooked streets and higgledy-piggledy houses, their sloping thatched roofs providing a ready perch for a dream fiddler? If it had ever been, Grodzisk was no longer the *shtetl* of imaginary homelands. There are no pious black-cloaked Jews here endlessly arguing points from the Talmud, not even a rebellious youth longing to escape to the enlightenment of the city. Of course,

I knew that. I know that. Yet the twinge of loss is there all the same.

We head for a side street where Peter Rytke has told us there is an archive. The address leads us to an old-fashioned bal-conied building which bears a sign announcing 'weddings'. Monica and I look at each other in perplexity and giggle as we dare the partly opened door. Inside, we find ourselves in a registry office which, with its darkly varnished furniture, array of flowers and leather-backed chairs, could be in England. A knock at a door produces a pert, young, short-haired and thoroughly modern woman, who tells us with a smile that she does indeed have a few minutes between weddings and yes, this is the Grodzisk Mazowiecki archive. I explain, through Monica, that I am looking for any traces there may be of the one-time Jewish community here, and any records they may have of my family. When she asks if I want birth certificates, I have a momentary aberration and say, yes, forgetting that though my mother grew up here, she wasn't in fact born here.

The young woman looks troubled. 'What year?' she asks politely.

I tell her and she suddenly explains that with Jews it's not so simple. Dates are fluid. Sometimes people registered their chil-dren in batches or years later or not at all.

I nod sagely, remembering my parents' own erratic accounts of their birth dates, and the inevitable vagaries of transposition from Hebrew calendar years to Christian ones. I also have a dis-tinct and recent image of my mother refusing to allow me to handle her passport as I filled out landing forms for the two of us, and then embarking on a complicated explanation of why the date of birth it displayed was not the one she had most often confessed to.

The young woman rushes on. She herself has only lived in Grodzisk for two years. The person who knows most about Jewish Grodzisk, an old man, is away. Away in China.

'China?' Monica and I echo and find ourselves on the verge of giggles again.

The woman nods and picks up the telephone. 'I'll just check.'

'Yes, China,' she confirms at the end of her conversation. 'He'll be back in about two weeks.' She tells us she will try to have a look in the archive while we walk, but she can't really tell us where to go, since she doesn't know.

No one else seems to know either. The history of Grodzisk with its once substantial Jewish population seems to be as deeply buried as Atlantis. We follow a newly printed map and walk towards what we assume may have been the old quarter and the ghetto, since the streets here are curved and irregular rather than grid-like. But the centre of town was partly destroyed in the first bombings of the war, together with the fountain which figures so largely in the narratives of my mother's generation as a communal meeting point. The old market square is now a renovated pedestrian precinct which spills over into a dusty field opposite a school advertising language teaching. Nor is there anything to indicate what the Jews called Shulgasse – synagogue street – not even a plaque to commemorate a vanished building, let alone my grandfather's school. The first preoccupation of the present inhabitants of Grodzisk is hardly their obliterated Jewry, herded into a ghetto on December 1, 1940 and then transported to the Warsaw Ghetto between the tenth and the fourteenth of February 1941 only finally to be sent to the Treblinka death camp.

But when we pass a graceful, Baroque church and find ourselves in a well-tended Catholic cemetery, I realise there is a different form of remembering going on here. A number of the newer and more elaborate tombstones, surrounded by fresh flowers, are monuments to those who lost their lives in the Warsaw Uprising of 1944. These are Polish heroes relegated to oblivion during the years of Communist rule, because their glorification would have reminded Poles that the Soviets were not always their loyal comrades. During the Warsaw Uprising, the Soviet army sat passively in the Praga suburb of the city and allowed the Poles to die in their thousands. The end of Communist rule has allowed wartime resistance heroes to be excavated from oblivion and to take their proper place in the pantheon of Polish nationalism. Amongst other things, memory is also a political tool in the building of nations.

We walk along in search of the wooden houses which would have characterised the Jewish quarter in my mother's day. There are none, but I snap a few pictures of older dilapidated stuccoed buildings in partly hidden courtyards. When I show these to my mother, after my return to London, in the hope that she will recognise her native streets, she gazes at the images with evident perplexity. 'Could be,' she says vaguely. 'Maybe . . .' The scale of early memory – when Grodzisk was to her the inflated centre of the universe – is missing. Everything in my pictures looks small and shabby. There is nothing here to recognise, except perhaps the train station, from where she left never to return.

Passing a bakery, Monica and I buy food for lunch and take it to a bench in the pedestrian precinct. Poised incongruously above a clothes shop, a large sign advertises 'Psychoterapia'. We consider this new Grodzisk, which now has psychotherapy but no Jews and certainly not Monica's father in it, and munch at our pastries.

Suddenly an old man cycles up to us and stops so close that his leg brushes my coat. His face is gnarled and toothless and unsmiling and his posture exudes hostility. He stares at us and stares and makes a guttural sound deep in his throat. The stare makes me feel not only foreign, but as alien as a Martian. Then he starts muttering, 'One is brown and the other is black.' He repeats this with a venomous chuckle. An abrupt certainty comes over me. I know that he knows we're Jewish and he doesn't like it one little bit. Fixed in that hostile stare, I feel the history which is my parents' edging closer and closer until I have to run. I am afraid. Would this buried racial fear choke me if there were nowhere to run to, if there were no solid British passport tucked in my bag?

'What's wrong?' Monica asks. She is immune to my particular ghosts and insists that the man was just commenting on the colour of our raincoats. Maybe she is right, but I can't shed the aura of malice he has generated. I suggest we give a miss to the Jewish cemetery which is some two miles distant on the other side of the tracks and head straight off for Pruszków. I have had a full description of this cemetery – which dates from the seventeenth century – from one of my parents' friends. I know of its desecration during the war, how its tombstones were ripped up and scattered and left lying or incorporated in road paving until well into the seventies, when a committee of foreign-based survivors sent funds for its restoration. None of my family is buried there. Nor, it seems, when we return to the gracious young woman at the registry, does any documentation exist for them amidst the town's public records. Personal memory apart, there is no trace of my maternal family's existence in Grodzisk.

The sky, when we arrive in Pruszków, is as grey as the looming charcoal bulk of the station. No visions of charming spa towns here, but a nineteenth-century industrial steeliness. Opposite the station there is a placard displaying a large map. We study it, looking for Ulica Kraszewskiego – the address noted on my father's card at the Historical Institute – and duly find it. The problem is that the map fails to tell us where we are or indicate the train station. For many years in Communist countries maps were not produced: the State did not consider knowledge of where things were a good thing. Far better for individuals to be unsure of their bearings or for foreigners not to know where important installations – like stations and tracks – could be found. The Poles are trying, but certain skills have not yet been perfected.

We ask a passing woman the way, but she merely points us towards a taxi rank. The driver we approach mutters, 'It's only a few minutes,' but he raises no finger to indicate the path, nor does he urge us on board. A second query doesn't help. '*Cham*,' Monica murmurs, as we start to walk in what we hope is the right direction.

It is a word she uses frequently during our Polish travels. It means 'boor' or 'peasant', a derogatory expletive which sums up the age-old and deeply Polish opposition between the cultivated or aristocratic and the vulgar, the unrefined. I tell Monica I have always thought the word *cham* was Yiddish, not Polish. No, she says, her parents used it all the time and they spoke no Yiddish. Later, when we ask various Poles, they confirm her view. I am not convinced and when I get back to London, I check it out. The word does indeed come from Yiddish and is used to designate a plebe or common man, unlearned, uncultured. In its plural, *chamoyn*, it means crowd or mass. This slippage between the languages is yet another instance of the osmosis between Polish and Polish-Jewish cultures, something that purists or nationalists on both sides would rather not acknowledge.

We walk along a leafy Victorian street of red-brick houses, past a large pencil factory with a shrine to a graceful pink and blue Madonna in its forecourt, and once again ask our way of a passerby. He shakes his head, points a finger in the opposite direction and rushes off.

Monica exclaims once more at the incivility of Poles in public spaces. This lack of simple politeness, let alone a graciousness towards strangers, casts a pall on our days. 'Why do they behave like this?' she moans. I give her my hypothesis, garnered after several visits to Moscow. Decades of living under Stalinist rule – the rule of informers and secret police – makes people wary. They interiorise suspicion. No one, certainly no one met in a public space, is to be trusted. Anyone might be an informer. So it's safer not to engage, not to meet people's eyes, certainly not to smile. Safer to rush along and away. Who knows who might be watching? 'The young should be different,' I say and we test my hypothesis by asking directions of a young woman. She smiles back at us and gives us full instructions before going off with a wave. Sometimes it's better not to have memory.

We are walking up a street of slightly dowdy shops. Beside one, a woman has spread her wares on the pavement – huge panniers of raspberries and dill. I sniff at them and again realise that the outdoor smells of rural Poland are familiar to me. Something about the odour of weeds in moist earth, of hidden blueberries, or fern, or plum and apple boughs heavy with fruit beckons to me. I had always assumed these were smells of the Canadian countryside, but they are here, now, on this street.

At the crossroads with the main road to Warsaw, we come upon a McDonald's so resplendent in its newness that it seems to light up both town and weather. There is an elaborate children's slide complete with tree house, a giant Ronald McDonald sitting on a bench, tables and chairs in freshly bright plastic to compete with parasols of throbbing red. As if we had suddenly developed a flagrant passion, we dash in, use pristine loos, order cappuccinos in paper cups and sit in the garden of tubular dazzle (where we can smoke) bemoaning our Western perversion, now in translation. In fact, everything is in translation: all the usual McDonald's signs here are in Polish and Monica takes pictures, as if she were Tarantino in a French Burger King.

We leave the light relief behind and find the street where the family textile firm had its premises. We are in the very heart of town. Nothing here has changed except for the names on the shopfronts. The vast red-brick Victorian church with its two steeples is intact and opposite it stands the row of two- and three-storey cream-stuccoed terraces some of which used to belong to the Borensztejns. I have been here before, but this time I have a more specific pre- and post-war address to visit.

The tree-lined Ulica Kraszewskiego flanks the side of the church square and runs south of it. It has a prosperous, tidy, one might have said bourgeois, feel. I am filled with anticipation as we follow the downward movement of the numbers. I have visions of myself knocking on the door, asking about the history of the house's inhabitants, sniffing through the rooms where I know from family story my brother first lived with my parents and the returning refugees gathered just after the war. But when we get to number thirteen, instead of a stone building like its neighbours, we see a leafy forecourt and behind it a large utilitarian sixties structure which bears the sign, 'Miejska Biblioteka Publiczna'. My parents' house has been torn down and replaced by a public library.

I swallow my disappointment. Yesterday's sense of entering a hall of mirrors comes back to me. The reflected face now bears a joker's malicious smile. I chase it away and console myself with the notion that my father might even be pleased to find that his home had been turned into a library. Maybe one of my own books has taken up residence there: my history of Cabaret, perhaps, translated into Polish some years after my father's death.

Monica and I retrace our steps. We pop into a shop on the

side of the church square and I notice how deep the back store-room is in comparison to the retail space. I envisage my grandmother as one of the three plump ladies who sit there and eye us without saying a word. We pass a park where I imagine my father engaging in one of his Sabbath games of barefoot football. But it is only when we are standing on the station plat-form that my own blindness kicks me in the groin. On the opposite side of the station from the town – the side that I hadn't taken in because I was sitting in the wrong place – lies the huge expanse of the railway yard and carriage works: a vast sprawl of old industrial buildings, barrack-like structures, warehouses, a tall thin smokestack, heaps of tracks, coal and gravel mounds. In front of them, perched on the rails like so many extras in a film set, stands a row of ancient carriages. The writing on them, now barely visible, spells out 'Pociąg Pogotowia Sieciowego Pruszków'. These are the trains which were sent out to rescue damaged ones on the line. This is the railway yard which once belonged to my great-grandfather, the very yard in which my father worked as slave labour to the Nazis. And more . . .

I walk the length of the platform and stare and imagine the wartime that I cannot see until the arrival of the Warsaw train obliterates my vision.

Wartime: 1939–41

Like a high-voltage wire, stretched ever more tautly between peace and war, the last weeks of August 1939 were electric with anticipation throughout Poland.

On the twenty-third, news of the German-Soviet non-aggression pact threw politicians and populace into a frenzy: Poland was once again sandwiched between her two ancient enemies. From the radio, Hitler's ever more raucous threats blared. Poland answered with staunch ones of its own. Its heroic army would never allow itself to taste defeat. The troops were mobilised. In the small town of Pruszków, shops and streets and the central market were busier than ever as people rushed to stock up on wood and coal, salt and sugar, emptying shelves and warehouses of their stores. The great grey bulk of the train station heaved with passengers waiting for trains which might have room for mere civilians. In the streets and behind houses, trenches were being dug. Cellars were sealed with sandbags. Stone walls which might serve to retain the enemy's poisonous gas were pulled down. The only imaginable shape for war was the previous one. There would be horses and artillery and trenches and mud and gas. The brave Poles would be victorious. The British would help. One could count on the British. And the French.

Everyone talked of war and made preparations, yet few believed it would really come. It was summer. It was hot. The Minister of Defence was still on holiday at the seaside. Without him, how could there be war?

In their apartment, a block away from the church square which faced the family textile firm, my father, Aron, a vigorous twenty-five-year-old, spent every spare minute glued to the radio or the newspapers – despite the fact that he had again quarrelled with his father and recently set up his own new enterprise. My mother, Hena, twenty-three, was more intent on her small son, Staszek – Sholem, in Yiddish, or peace. He was two and half months old and he had been named in hope. But on Thursday the thirty-first, when the local chemist started handing out gas masks and told her he had none to fit her child, hope seemed in short supply.

Early the next morning, the sirens set up their blare. The air was suddenly filled with the din of planes. From the distance came the rumble of explosions and the sound of artillery. The family, together with the other residents of the apartment building, huddled in a makeshift shelter in the cellar. In moments of quiet, they surged into the streets, newly crowded with people fleeing areas that had suffered direct hits. There was news that a bomb had fallen in the centre of Grodzisk where Hena's parents lived.

By the third day of war, Hena's milk had ceased to flow. After a hasty consultation, Aron set out for Grodzisk. The telephone lines were down and Hena needed to know what state her parents were in. She wanted them by her side. It was only sixteen kilometres away, but the going was slow. Trains were for soldiers and most motorised vehicles had been seized for military use. Aron walked. The roads teemed. The movement of tanks and military vehicles, the occasional bomb probably intended for the fiercely defended capital, forced one into detours through neighbouring fields. When he reached the town which had lost its centre, Aron found his in-laws thankfully safe. Hena's best friend, however, was dead, killed outright by the bomb and its only fatality. He hated to have to bring her that news. She was already anxious enough and needed all her strength for the child. On top of it all, David Lipszyc, a responsible elder, was reluctant to leave his flock. Aron protested. Sara, his mother-in-law, protested even more loudly in a stubborn tone he had never heard her use to her husband before. Bad enough, she said, that she didn't know whether her son was dead or alive. But she had to go to her daughter and her grandson. Family came first.

By the next day, they had gathered a few belongings together. For an exorbitant fee, my father found a peasant willing to transport them in his cart. They reached Pruszków by nightfall, shaken but intact, and moved in with Hena and Aron. Not for long.

From the radio came repeated declarations that the brave Polish army would never give up Warsaw. All its might was concentrated in defence of the glorious capital. Believing what they heard, my parents determined that Warsaw would be safer than an unimportant town like Pruszków. They set out for the capital. It was not a wise move. Wisdom goes hand in hand with a sense of habitual reality and Warsaw was a disaster zone of a kind no one had imagined. Something utterly new and unforeseen was happening. Devastation came from the skies. In the blink of an eye, squat, solid buildings, whole streets turned to rubble. Fire, smoke and acrid dust made air as unbreathable as the anticipated poisonous fumes. The dying and the wounded lay everywhere. Few hospitals remained untouched by bombs. There was neither water nor electricity. The dead horses of the Polish cavalry served as food. People ran out of shelters with knives to gouge chunks out of them and then scurried back into hiding. My mother banged on closed shop doors in search of milk for her son.

At the first lull, the family headed back for Pruszków. They joined an exodus of refugees fleeing the city. Starving, battered, they moved in crowded peasant wagons, in dilapidated trucks or on foot. They carried bundles or pushed prams unsteady with crying children and hastily gathered possessions. Rumours flew in all directions. The British were coming – it would all soon be over. This town was safe and that one was not. No, no, that town had been razed to the ground, everyone shot. No . . .

There were also graphic accounts of the horror perpetrated on Jews. Of Jews flayed and cursed by Gentiles who held them responsible for the bombs which exploded all around them. Of German soldiers whipping and torturing rabbis and scholars, cutting or pulling their beards from their faces together with strips of raw flesh. Of public and clamorous executions of Jews who had refused to deny their faith. Of equally quick killing of anyone who stepped forward to help them. Of Jews whipped for wearing their ritual prayer shawls. Of others forced to use sanctified garments or pages ripped from holy books to clean toilets or floors or cars.

Confusion, terror, ran as rampantly through the streets as rumour in those first three weeks of war. No one – neither politicians, nor military, nor ordinary people – knew which turn to take. Almost devoid of modern arms and poorly deployed, attacked from three sides at once by Panzer divisions, the Polish military fought with romantic valour. German casualties were even heavier than in the far longer campaign against France. But spirited bravery could do little against a German army of 1,850,000 men equipped with 2,800 tanks – outnumbering the Poles ten to one – and more than 2,000 planes. The daily wishful rumours that the British were coming or were already bombing Germany bore no truth. Blitzkrieg was triumphant. On September 27, Warsaw fell: over 200,000 Poles and Jews were dead or wounded and some 20,000 had been taken prisoner.

The war from the skies had a certain anonymity. It could almost take its place with natural disaster. The war on the ground was both more human and more brutal. In its beatings and executions, it had a visceral sadism. It was calculated to humiliate, to reduce its victims to abject obedience. Psychological terror went hand in hand with military might. Hitler's injunction authorised killing 'without pity or mercy of all men, women and children'. Jews were first in line, closely followed by Polish professionals and intellectuals. What remained of Poland's population could, until

Germany's necessary 'living space' was ultimately won, serve as a vast and cheap labour force in the Nazi war effort. Only gradually did all this become clear.

On October 5, Hitler headed the victory parade into Warsaw. He made no secret of his plans for Poland. The contemptible foster child of the corrupt Western democracies would soon be 'swept off the face of the earth'. In the meantime, the rich industrialised north and west of Poland were to be annexed to the Reich and Germanised. Schools were closed. Polish was forbidden as a public language, together with all cultural activity. The professional and 'possessing' classes, both Polish and Jewish, were executed or deported to the territory of the newly formed General Government which ruled the rest of German-occupied Poland. This area, with a population of over twelve million, was to be run under martial law and exploited for its human and natural resources. Krakow was its capital. Warsaw was destined to be transformed into a small German colony.

By now, the Soviet army had established its dominance on all territory east of the River Bug. This region held twelve million people, two million of whom were soon to be deported as forced labour to mines and lumber camps in the Soviet north and east. Poland stood defeated and partitioned along the line of the river. The Polish government set up in exile, first in Romania, then in Paris and finally in London.

German military control of Poland lasted until October 25. If the German military brought devastation, the occupation that was to follow proved even worse. Behind the front-line troops came the Einsatzgruppen, the special execution squads drawn from the ranks of the SS, whose task was not only to quell resistance, but to slaughter whole categories of the population. This needed a little time to unfold in its full horror: in the next few years half of Poland's doctors, lawyers and engineers would be killed, forty per cent of its professors, eighteen per cent of its priests. Whole villages were to be burnt to the ground in retribution for partisan activity. Three million Jews – some ninety per cent of the Jewish-Polish population – were to be murdered in the camps or ghettos or in haphazard Nazi terror. By the end of the war some three million 'non-Jewish' Poles had also lost their lives.

The small town of Pruszków suffered no direct bombing. It took the Germans under a week to rout the tiny Polish army contingent and establish Nazi rule. They moved into the best houses and the town hall and in a reign of terror beat the townspeople into subservience. The local *beysme dresh* could hold no more religious services. Transformed into a crowded refugee centre and soup kitchen for the poor, its wooden walls reverberated with news from the surrounding area and the sobbing of women and children.

With its small and relatively Westernised Jewish population, Pruszków fared marginally better than the more traditional *shtetls*. None the less, most Poles knew who the Jews were and which businesses belonged to them. Jewish shops were looted, their goods taken by the Germans or, at least at first, when examples needed to be made in the institution of terror, randomly distributed to Gentiles. Using the excuse of her baby, my mother kept the family premises closed as much as possible. Sometimes the Germans were kind about children and my mother could get by in the language. Her sister-in-law, Rosa, asked her if she could borrow Staszek, so that she too could have an excuse for keeping her business closed – an act prohibited by the Germans. Without stock, there would be starvation. Prices had already begun to rise wildly. Bread and meat and flour were in short supply. Salt had vanished. Most of the peasants who brought in their produce from the surrounding countryside would now take only goods in exchange. Money had lost its value. Whole days could be spent in the activity of barter and the hunt for basic foodstuffs. When rationing began in December 1939, the coupons for Poles provided only for some 600 calories, a quarter of an adult's daily needs. On top of it all, the winter of '39–'40 was one of the bitterest ever, with temperatures diving down to –40 degrees centigrade. Coal quickly grew scarce. One had to go further and further out of town to find wood.

Like most Jewish men, my father kept a low profile, staying indoors as much as possible during the day. He was perpetually alert to the sound of marching boots. Their rhythmic clatter over cobblestones, their mounting resonance on wooden stairs, became for him the essential sound of war. Throughout his life, he never successfully inoculated himself against that sound, which produced a racing heart, clenched fists, a burst of perspiration.

The labour round-ups began. An unexpected knock on the door signalled a brutal search followed by a forced march to a work site, which in its barbarous conditions could just as easily

prove a death site. Fear became the dominant emotion.
Survival entailed cunning. Realising that in the crowds of
Warsaw he would be less easily recognised as Jewish, Aron
started to take the trolley into the city. Here he renewed his
contacts with the textile manufacturers and importers who
were his business acquaintances and sometimes relatives. One
of these told him that rather than find his entire stock in the
hands of Germans, he would give it over to my father and the
relative safety of Pruszków. Payment could be made after the
war. He trusted him. And in any event, it wouldn't be that long
now. It couldn't take that long.

Everyone still believed the British would soon be coming.

Slowly, carefully, Aron began to transport reels of cloth. One
by one, wrapped in brown paper and held under his arm in the
trolley, Harris tweeds, Manchester woollens and cottons made
their way from Warsaw to Pruszków. I can see his features,
forced into nonchalance, his eyes wary despite himself, his posture rigidly casual, as he pretends he is carrying out an ordinary
activity. Once or twice, a larger shipment was organised, a car
and driver found and successfully bribed.

By the end of 1939, bribery was already quickly becoming a
way of life. Poles could be bribed and Polish policemen could
be bribed – to look the other way, to serve as couriers, to conceal a Jew for a short time, to accomplish a variety of small or
larger tasks. The difficulty was always that they might up the
agreed amount, or take everything that there was to take, using
the threat of exposure to the Germans as a bargaining tool.
When the ghettos came into being towards the autumn of 1940
and with them a Jewish police force, Jews too could be bribed.

With the textile hoard safely in Pruszków, the problem arose of where to conceal it. Subject to looting, shops were precarious. Subject to searches, home was even more so. My maternal grandfather came up with a solution. On the roof of their block of flats there was an old unused cistern. Its top could be reached with a ladder. Late one night, well after curfew, the reels of cloth were silently shunted on to the roof and flung one by one into the tank. This cache of goods turned into a veritable treasure. The rarity of cloth during the war so transformed its value, that the stocked cistern proved a far better safety-deposit box than a Swiss bank account.

Probably towards the end of November '39, my mother's brother arrived in Pruszków. Adolf Lipszyc, Adek for short, had served as a lieutenant in the Polish army. (Though the figure is not generally known, there were 150,000 Jewish servicemen in Poland at the outbreak of war, of whom around 33,000 were killed in the first month of fighting.) In the battle on the Eastern Front, he shed his uniform when it became clear that it jeopardised his life. The invading Russians, as the Katyn massacre fatefully proved, were only too ready to execute officers rather than abide by prisoner-of-war regulations.

Although Adek could replace his uniform, he couldn't rid himself of his military boots quickly enough. Spotted by a Russian officer, he was arrested. His claim to have stolen the boots served no purpose. Forced to hand over his papers, he realised his fate was sealed. In the few moments that his interrogator turned his back on him and stepped into the next room to have the papers translated and checked, Adek leapt through a window and ran. He ran and ran, darted through alleys, slowed his pace in the crowded town centre, ran again until, exhausted, he stopped at the edge of a village and knocked at a peasant's hut.

By all accounts – and especially my mother's – Adek was not only tall and blond and handsome, but persuasive, daring, quick-witted and above all, authoritative. A graduate in chemistry from the University of Vienna, he spoke fluent German and had seen something of the world.

Now, he explained his situation as a fleeing officer to the peasant and enlisted his help. A pair of ordinary shoes was duly found to replace the tell-tale boots. Soup and bread were proffered. Then Adek was once more on his way. He slept rough, under the shelter of trees or in barns or sometimes didn't sleep at all. He was one of thousands moving across the country, fleeing, uncertain of a destination.

No one seems to know Adek's exact trajectory from Eastern Poland to Warsaw and its outskirts. At some point he must have had to cross the River Bug, which divided Russian- from German-occupied Poland. The river was a highly patrolled frontier, treacherous to cross without the necessary passes stamped and checked by authorities on either side. It is probable that Adek did not yet have any identity papers. So he would have had to bribe one of the boatmen who smuggled people fleeing in either direction across the frontier, under the shield of night. These boatmen, as a friend of my parents', Jonas Sebrien, told me, were more perfidious than Charon. They would agree a sum for the crossing and then rob their passengers mid-river, stripping them of everything including,

more often than not, their lives. From the banks, waiting passengers would hear the cries and moans of attacked women and
beaten men. Jonas himself made the passage with his brother.
As soon as they had moved a little way from shore and the
boatman began to threaten them, they jumped him, took over
the oars, and only released him when they reached the opposite shore.

At some point in his hazardous journey across Poland, Adek
acquired new papers and perhaps a temporary identity. The
story goes that he met a young woman en route and struck up
a conversation with her. They grew friendly. The woman told
him her father was a station-master and could arrange a travel
permit and passable identification papers for Adek. But the rail
pass was not an immediate boon. Train travel could prove
slower than journeying on foot. Freight cars were jammed with
prisoners of war; passenger cars carried mostly Germans. The
wait for engines seemed eternal and when one arrived, five
miles an hour was the average speed. Bombed rails made stops
long and frequent.

While he was waiting for his travel papers, or soon after – in
any case, on the German side of the new frontier – Adek began
to witness the atrocities which determined his wartime choices.
He saw Jewish children heaved into ditches by Nazi soldiers
and summarily shot. He saw a straggling line of some hundred
Jewish men, their clothes in tatters, forced by pistol-bearing
soldiers to run up a hill. All the while, the Jews were made to
intone, as if it were a marching chant, 'Jews are swine', 'Jews are
swine'. When one of them fell over, or faltered in his pace, he
was pistol-whipped across ears and head, or kicked until the

blood flowed. The faces of the old men were anguished. The young wept silently. The onlookers were stunned: women crossed themselves as they gazed on the sorry cavalcade. Dizzy with their own power, young, fresh-faced Germans whipped abject Jews into a performance of callisthenics on the central square. By evening, not a single Jew in that group remained alive. There were only corpses heaped like rag dolls on to peasant carts. The next day Adek's fury overcame his fear: he punched a Nazi soldier who was tugging an old rabbi by the beard. The surprise of the attack gave Adek an advantage. He beat the soldier to the ground, hustled the old man into a doorway, and ran.

By the time he reached the family in Pruszków, Adek's mind was made up.

I imagine the scene of the family reunion in the apartment in Pruszków. The curtains are tightly drawn. There is a small fire burning behind the grate. A candle at the centre of the dinner table sheds a desultory light. My grandmother, Sara, weeps. She weeps with joy because her son is alive and with her. She weeps in distress because of the news he brings. She urges him to eat. My father paces and smokes, his ears ever alert to the sounds on the staircase. He thinks his own mother, Estera, did well to die peacefully the preceding year, ahead of this torrent of violent deaths. My mother clasps her baby tightly to her and murmurs a lullaby filled with those age-old nursery warnings which are as nothing compared to their present plight. My grandfather runs his fingers through his blond beard and considers. Adek's words are adamant. David is proud of his son, proud of his military bearing, his certainty, his boldness – even of his occasional rashness. But he doesn't think he can agree with him now.

Adek is telling them that their only hope of survival is to bury their Jewishness and pretend to be Poles. They will go to Warsaw. Not a word of Yiddish is to pass their lips, no gesture, nor prayer which might betray who they are.

David shakes his head. Things are bad, he says. But things have been bad before. Pogroms are nothing new. They will overcome this one too. It is wrong to pretend to be something one isn't. It is a breach of the commandments to deny one's Jewishness. God will provide.

Adek bristles. His father is getting old. He doesn't understand the modern world, the enormity that is at hand. He doesn't understand the cruel ferocity of the Nazis, the racial beliefs that underpin their savagery towards the Jews. This is not some random pogrom unleashed by Russian peasants. The entire might of the German military machine is being brought into play here to cleanse the expanding Reich of what it sees as subspecies, first in order of which are Jews. Adek understands that. He began to understand it while he was studying in Vienna. He understands it even better after these few shattering weeks of war. He also knows that the only thing the Germans respect is an aura of power. Jews are scum whom they expect to lower their eyes and bleat timidly. Like scum, they can be wiped away without a thought. The only way to outwit the Germans is to beat them at their own game. He has already done it a few times on his way here, sitting squarely on his train seat, brazening it out, treating Germans with that lofty assurance their stereotyped Jew

could never dare match. He argues with his father. He looks
to his friend Aron for support.

My father is uncertain. All his capital is tied up here. There
is his baby boy to consider. Warsaw is no place for an infant.
Secretly, he doubts that he can match Adek's authority and
masquerade as something he isn't. He is no actor.

'I'm not going anywhere without our parents,' my mother
states.

Adek shrugs and leaves them the next day. But his words resonate through the family. They have hardly been unaware that,
despite their indiscriminate killing and torture of both Poles
and Jews, it is the Jews the new Nazi masters have singled out.
Prohibitive laws are aimed at their religion, and at their very
being. Many of the Nazi edicts are couched in language
designed to surround Jews with an aura of filth and transmit-
table illness, particularly sexual illness. As Jews, they are agents
of plague.

Communal prayer was first to be banned. Then a law was
imposed prohibiting the ritual slaughter of meat. Jewish businesses are now forced to stay open on the Sabbath; this too
is the key day for forced labour round-ups. The *mikvehs* – the
ritual bath houses – are under attack in Warsaw as purported
breeding grounds for epidemic disease. By December they will
all be closed and Warsaw's Jewish women will begin to pour
into Pruszków to use the baths here, until the use of these, too,
is prohibited.

The family decide that, given my grandmother's piety and
her insistence on following all laws to the letter, it would be
more secure for her and David, strangers in Pruszków, to have

their own accommodation. A small house with a garden and a space for chickens is found for them on the edge of town. Here Sara can practise her rituals in relative obscurity. Just in case …

A freezing 1940 dawned and still the British hadn't arrived. Instead the Nazis had been working hard at consolidating their regime – creating a rigid hierarchy of bureaucratic and disciplinary authority – with the SS at the top, moving down through the Polish police to the Jewish councils and eventually the Jewish police at the bottom. Life was governed by passes which the police repeatedly checked. In this occupied state, the most important enterprises and estates had been turned over to Germans or *Volksdeutsche* (the Polish citizens of German origin), for whom Poles and Jews functioned as slave labour. There had been an influx too, particularly in Warsaw and the larger towns, of German doctors and dentists and a variety of professionals to service the new regime. For the native population, life had become a daily struggle for subsistence. In real terms, wages spiralled downward to a tenth of their original value. It cost some 1,500 zloty to feed a family of four for a month, but most workers could earn only between 100–300 zloty.

Despite the repeated instances of terror and brutality, the proliferation of laws to subjugate and humiliate the Jewish population in particular, in Pruszków and Warsaw an aura of weird normality gradually replaced panic. Normality, after all, is a function of habit, and most habits now centred on the procuring of food and heat and on evading the grip of authority. For my father, it was normal to be constantly on the alert,

to weave a route through lanes and back alleys at the sight of
a uniform or to leap through windows and dash into cellars. It
was normal to bribe and to huddle in secret places for prayer
or conversation with friends. It was normal to be subjected to
haphazard violence or blackmail.

In the midst of all this, my mother discovered that she was
pregnant.

'Yes, pregnant! Can you believe it?'

Her dismay, when she tells me about this, is palpable.

'These were hardly times in which to have another child.
And I was so ignorant, so impossibly stupid about . . .'

She waves her hand to hide her continuing discomfort about
words like contraception. Her lips tremble as she recounts
how she secretly went to see a gynaecologist in Warsaw, a man
who was a friend of her father's. Somehow, a miscarriage was
induced.

This episode which still bears its quantum of shame is one
she has only ever talked about when pressed and then only to
contradict my brother's conjecture that she had suffered a still-
birth. She whispers its telling and the whisper gathers
embarrassment as she notes that the same doctor explained the
mysteries of contraception to her, something for which she was
always grateful.

While my mother tended what there was to tend of business,
my father surreptitiously visited Adek in Warsaw. In order to
travel by train rather than trolley, he now had to go to the local
doctor and procure a lice pass which certified that he had been

vaccinated against lice. This was the latest form of humiliation inflicted on Jews. He also had to show a permit naming a place of employment. This he didn't yet have. Soon, as a Jew, he would no longer be permitted to travel by train at all.

Adek had recently married the daughter of a former Jewish associate. He had also set up a cosmetics firm which was doing a thriving business selling beauty products – creams and soaps and perfumes – under a variety of labels to the new influx of war rich. He manufactured these himself in a warehouse laboratory. He had begun to make friends in high places. He was now Adolf Hiszczynski. An Aryan.

There were several methods of procuring an 'Aryan' identity and dissimulating one's Jewishness. None of them was straightforward. All of them required a brazen confidence. Before the age of photocopying, when a baptismal certificate was lost, a typed replacement could be got from the church which had first issued it. In order to become official, this replacement had then to be stamped by a registered notary. The Jew in search of an 'Aryan' identity needed first to find a plausible name, then the name of a destroyed church and for good measure, the name of a dead priest. Next, he needed to type out a baptismal certificate containing this information and have it authorised by a tame notary or an engraver who could create a good imitation of a notary's stamp – all for a fee, of course. Armed with all this, plus a great deal of composure and a good story to explain the loss of the original baptismal certificate, he could then register with the police and obtain the *Kennkarte* – the German-issued ID every Gentile had to carry.

An alternative method was to gather all the information on

place, date of birth, names of parents and godparents and baptismal priest of a Gentile killed in the war, travel to the church
where the original baptismal certificates were kept and claim to
be this person. It was best in this case to address oneself to a
young priest whose memory was short. These 'authentic' certificates were, of course, the safest.

The simplest, but not always the most secure method, was
to purchase one of the blank baptismal certificates created by
the clergy for sale on the black market. All that was then
needed was to fill out a name, forge a stamp and achieve a semblance of an original. The trickiness here was that the issuing
church could be checked for records.

During the years of the war Adek procured Aryan identities
for at least several dozen Jews. He used all of these methods and
others.

Sometime in the spring of 1940, perhaps earlier, the anticipated
boots finally arrived and marched my father away to do forced
labour. He was sent to work in the very rail repair yard that had
once belonged to his grandfather, now called Zakłady
Naprawcze Taboru Kolejowego. We know very little about his
experience there except that the humiliation and brutality he
endured made him unwilling or unable to talk about it. My
brother claims that Aron's strength and toughness permitted
him to rise to head the rail-laying brigade. We don't know for
certain. But at such work sites, a man worked until he dropped
and when he dropped he was beaten and worked some more.
Human hides grew thick and scarred from whipping; the food
ration was far less than enough to sustain a man and usually

amounted to bread and watery soup on good days. Nor do we know for certain how long were the stretches Aron spent away from home. He was fortunate not to be one of the 180 men selected to work on the site after the remainder of the Pruszków Jewish population were transported to the Warsaw Ghetto: all of these 180 were either deported directly to Treblinka or executed in front of the brickworks.

My niece Abigail, who as a child in Canada was very close to my father, told me a story which bears witness to the grimness of my father's labour camp experience – something he never spoke about to me. She was around ten or eleven and writing a school project on the Second World War while her grandpa and younger brother, David, were in the room. Aron started to talk to them about faeces – the kind that were good to eat and the kind that weren't. Only animal faeces, he said, were edible. Human shit didn't have enough nutrients in it to make it worthwhile. So one had to scour the fields.

Abigail and David began to laugh and giggle over this disquisition on shit. Aron turned pale, ceased to speak and soon left the room.

The children hadn't understood then that he had been talking about the animal condition war had reduced him to, the terrible nature and degree of wartime hunger, the humiliation of an existence in which one became an expert on shit.

There is something emblematic about this scene. It goes some way towards explaining my father's silence about his wartime experience. If you speak, not only are you forced to remember, but you meet with the incredulity of listeners. The incommensurability of wartime atrocities spoken of in the safety of an ordinary front room can seem like delirium or exaggeration. Primo Levi, that most delicate and wise of survivors to have borne literary witness to Auschwitz, notes in *The Drowned and the Saved* how so many camp inmates 'remember a dream which frequently recurred during the nights of imprisonment: . . . they had returned home and with passion and relief were describing their past sufferings, addressing themselves to a loved person, and were not believed, indeed were not even listened to.'

Too often, this dream came true.

Largely, my father remained silent. His gestures, his displaced outbursts of rage, spoke for him.

In April 1940, brick walls started to go up on Marsalkowska Street, a central thoroughfare of Warsaw, as well as in the city's Jewish quarter. At first few Warsawians knew the purpose of these walls. By June it became clear. Jews were to be herded into the walled-off zone and Gentiles removed. There were some thirty miles of wall, ten foot high, topped with shards of glass and barbed wire. The ghetto had been created. On Yom Kippur, the Day of Atonement, of September 1940, loud-speakers throughout Warsaw ordered all remaining Jews to leave their homes and move into the ghetto limits by October 31.

By this time most towns and all cities in Poland had their own ghettos, their walls or barbed-wire fences and their entrances heavily patrolled by a hierarchy of guards. At first the walls were permeable. With the requisite passes, Jews and Poles could go in and out. On November 20, 1940, the Warsaw Ghetto was sealed from the inside. Poles could come in and out, but Jews could only come in. Without special dispensation – work and travel permits signed by the Judenrat, the ghetto's Jewish Council, and authorised by German authority – they would never put the ghetto walls 'legally' behind them again, except to travel to their death. By the following week, Poles were prohibited entry, too. To begin with, 160,000 men, women and children were crammed into the Warsaw Ghetto. Perversely, as the population rose with the influx of refugees and transportations from other ghettos – the figure reached 500,000 by early 1942 – the Germans progressively shrank the size of the ghetto itself. Single houses could contain up to 1,000 inhabitants. Needless to say, conditions were appalling. By the summer of 1941, with executions, poverty, overcrowding, starvation and epidemics, the monthly death toll was around 5,500.

In Pruszków, an open ghetto – one which permitted a flow of people between 8 a.m. and 6 p.m. – was established between October 10 and 12, 1940. My entire family, apart from Uncle Adek, lived within its cramped, insalubrious confines, four or five people to a room, seven to eight families in each flat. Since the local prayer hall was outside the ghetto area, the community elders decided to dismantle its wooden walls and rebuild it within the ghetto. When this proved impossible, they used the wood to heat the soup kitchen in winter. The six Torah scrolls were hidden in private houses. One of these may have gone to my grandfather, Reuben, still a relatively wealthy man, who now increasingly used his resources for charitable works. Despite the fall of France in June 1940, the consensus – in those vociferous night-time discussions which were all that remained to ghettoised Jews for enjoyment – was still that the war could go on for no more than another year. God forbid, my grandfather David used to say, repeating one of the witticisms of the time, that the war last as long as the Jews are capable of enduring!

Early one morning in January 1941, the loud-speakers blared that all Jews were immediately to gather with whatever possessions they could carry in the central square of the Pruszków Ghetto, men on one side, women on the other. Panic clutched at Hena: Aron wasn't there. Hastily she wrapped a few things in a bundle, exchanged hurried words with her parents, and Staszek in her arms, raced down to the street to search for him amidst the noisy, gathering crowd. Aron couldn't fend without her, of that she was certain. She approached Jewish Council members, Polish policemen, and then one Nazi guard after another – all to no avail. It was bitterly cold. Snow covered the ground. One of the SS guards took pity on her and told her to wait inside a house. The men were being sent off first.

She watched them being herded on to the waiting trucks. No Aron. There were a few coaches too. She spied her mother being prodded on to one and tried to push her way towards her. Too late. As the coach pulled away she had the terrible feeling that she might never see any of her family again.

Ever attuned to her anxiety, Staszek started to cry. She ruffled his curly blond hair, comforted him and with a forced smile tugged his hat down over his ears. Weren't they lucky to have such warm clothes. And good boots. Nice boots. They'd be useful on the trip. An adventure. Yes, a surprise voyage. On a coach. Of course, they would travel by coach.

After a last desperate look round for Aron, Hena confronted an official she knew slightly, and in her blithe and charming way, insisted that she and her little one had to be given a place on a coach, not a truck. How else was she to hold the child?

The precious seats were granted and the coach hurtled and juddered its way towards Warsaw, stopping at last in front of the ghetto gates amidst a frightened and bewildered crowd. Men in uniform, guns at the ready, barked orders, pistol-lashed the recalcitrant. Hena shrank back into her seat, crooned softly to Staszek. Suddenly, from the open door of the coach, she heard her name called. She lifted Staszek and moved forward slowly, only to find herself whipped away into a waiting car by a Polish policeman. 'On the orders of Pan Hiszczynski,' was all he said before depositing them at the door of her brother, Adek's house.

The house was luxurious. There were large, lavish rooms, made for entertaining; plush carpets and sofas and gleaming tables. There was food and drink of every description served in crystal goblets. Staszek gorged himself on fresh anchovies. After the hardship of Pruszków, Hena was grateful, but anxious. What of her parents? What of Aron? She wept. Her brother consoled her with the promise that he would get them out of the ghetto in due course. Nothing was insurmountable – as long as they all played the game as it needed to be played. The only thing Hena had to remember was that in this house, whenever there was anyone present aside from himself, his pregnant wife and his baby son, no reference was ever to be made to Jews. If the subject came up in conversation, her tone must always be derogatory. She was now Hena Hiszczynska, his sister, visiting from their estate in the countryside. All she needed to do was to dress beautifully, smile and look cheerful. This last was an absolute whenever there were guests in the house.

And there were many guests. Adek, known to his new friends as Max – the nickname he had acquired in Vienna – entertained in prodigal fashion. Wealthy Poles, German businessmen, professionals and even officers came to the house. Alcohol was downed in quantities, feasts prepared. The house whirled with an extravagance of gaiety. And an abundance of information.

Adek seemed to have his finger on every pulse. He knew about the progress of the war abroad and about Gestapo plans and movements at home. He knew the date when the Pruszków Ghetto was to be evacuated and soon he knew where his parents were housed in the Warsaw Ghetto. His contacts were everywhere. He had links with the carpetbaggers who could provide precious supplies for his cosmetics business – supplies undoubtedly pilfered from German factories. He knew whom to send to the countryside and where to purchase food from peasants. He knew forgers and suppliers of every kind of document. More importantly, he knew who was reliable and at what price. He may already have had links with the Home Army, the Armia Krajowa. He certainly had the influence in high quarters that charm and prodigality and not a little boldness bring. He used them all. Survival in wartime was a matter of breaking laws and Adek was an adept law-breaker and bender.

In that he was hardly alone. The entire population of the region was engaged in black-marketeering of some kind. Since salaries could not sustain life, this was an essential activity. Anyone who had a room or pallet to rent, did so. Smugglers haunted darkened or lonely stretches of the Warsaw Ghetto wall and exchanged basic supplies for valuables. Bribes were taken and bribes were given – by policemen and Judenrat offi-cials, by priests and landlords, by anyone with power or money. All this was accepted amongst an occupied people. Only black-mailers were despised – those who threatened acceptable law-breakers, such as smugglers, escapees from the ghetto, the Poles who advertently or inadvertently housed them, with exposure to the Germans and extorted funds. So rampant and abhorrent was this particular trade that in 1943, the under-ground Home Army, the AK, issued a directive condemning it and warning that blackmailers would be prosecuted before 'the court of Reborn Poland' after the war.

Adek used his network and expertise not only for his own survival, but to help others. One room in his factory was boarded up behind a false wall. Within it lived a succession of in-laws, relatives, friends and other Jews whom he had smug-gled out of the ghetto. They stayed there until documents and alternative accommodation could be assured. At night, the walled inhabitants of the factory were free to move around in the larger space.

One day, the premises' janitor complained to Adek of

strange night-time noises – creaking doors, shuffling feet, a murmur of voices. The building was haunted. He was frightened. Something had to be done. With a stern look, Adek warned him that if he continued thinking and talking like this, he would end up in a madhouse and everyone knew what the Germans did to the mentally ill. None the less, he swiftly organised new premises for the building's secret inhabitants. He rented an unused warehouse, set it up under the cosmetic firm's aegis, put in a few vanloads of products for cover and moved in 'his Jews'. It was here my father was eventually to come.

Meanwhile, however, there was the question of David and Sara. Sometime towards the end of February 1941, the necessary arrangements were in place. Early in the morning – at the time when German officers and Polish policemen at the ghetto wall were busy with the monitoring of the labour shifts which brought selected ghetto inhabitants in brutally policed groups to work sites throughout the city – a large gleaming car pulled up by the gates. Hena and little Staszek sat on its leather seats and watched as Adek, dressed in his long, belted, black leather coat, strode forward. His high and well-polished boots pounded the pavement. With his assertive gait and gestures, his blond head, he looked like a high-ranking SS officer. He passed some documents over to a guard and tapped his foot impatiently. From the car, they could almost make out the bark of his voice in German, ordering, not asking.

Some ten minutes later, though it felt like an eternity to Hena, David and Sara walked through the gate. Adek ushered them unhurriedly towards the car, prodding them just a little roughly as they got in: they were, after all, mere Jewish labour.

Then they drove away. They drove some 100 km south-east of Warsaw to Adamov, a small town in the Lublin area.

No one seems to know exactly what Adek's ploy was in retrieving his parents from the ghetto. It is likely that the procured documents claimed that these people were needed for labour – perhaps a particular chemical expertise necessary for the running of his enterprise. Whatever the ruse, it had its desired result. Four members of his immediate family were free.

Adamov was chosen because my grandmother had a brother there. The family moved in with him and led a quiet, unobtrusive life. Adamov was not important enough to warrant a strong German presence. The Nazis in any event were busy elsewhere. In June 1941, they invaded the Soviet Union. After the Russians had left, the Poles grew more sympathetic to the immured Jews – always potential Communist supporters in Polish eyes. Then, too, the labour round-ups were at a momentary lull. Within the confines of the small Adamov Ghetto, life ticked over in that relative misery and heightened anxiety which had become the norm. Until winter brought a typhus epidemic.

Typhus is an ugly disease. One of the so-called filth diseases, it is known variously as jail fever, war fever, or camp fever – all of which point to the dire conditions of overcrowding, underwashing and poor nourishment in which it spreads with epidemic swiftness, the affected lice leaping from body to body, as one grows too hot with fever, the other too cold with death. It was typhus which joined with 'General Winter' to turn Napoleon's Russian invasion into a rout: 30,000 cases were left to die in Vilna alone. During the Second World War, typhus plagued ghettos and concentration camps alike. Typically, the disease begins with headache, rash and high fever, producing a swelling of limbs and a darkening of the face. This is followed by gangrene and its attendant stench, delirium, the stupor from which the disease gets its name, and finally coma and death.

My mother came down with it first in the family. Her father nursed her, as, in his goodness, he nursed all neighbours and friends, providing solace as he could. My mother improved. She was young. Her father cured her, she has always claimed. And then David himself was afflicted. He struggled against the disease to no avail. By the end of the year, he was dead. Almost his last words were to the effect that he didn't mind dying now. The German armies had been halted at Moscow. The war really couldn't last much longer.

He gave his grandson his regimental pocket watch and ruby ring. On his daughter, paradoxically, his passing bestowed freedom.

My mother was desolate at his death, felt responsible for it, felt he had died for her. She still feels that, still talks of his passing with tears. It comes to me that her current bouts of obsessive preoccupation with what she calls the 'blackness' of her face may be a fuzzy memory of the blackening which typhus inflicts, the blackening in death of her father's face.

She says that with David's death, she no longer cared about anything, not even a God who would permit such injustice.

Nor was she afraid of anything.

Her father's death released her. It released her from being a good girl. It also released her from Jewishness. Within weeks, she had packed up a few belongings, and she, her reluctant mother and little Staszek were off to Warsaw, off to masquerade as Poles. Off to a life as Aryans. A slip of the Aryan mask to reveal the Jew beneath would mean death.

On Site

In its entry on Auschwitz, site and symbol of the Holocaust, my 1997 English-language *Insight Compact Guide to Poland*, provides a telling, if inadvertent, commentary on the tangled relations of Poles and Jews since the war.

First of all, there are the photographs. One is a rather picturesque shot of the main gate to Auschwitz capped by the curving wrought-iron letters which spell out 'Arbeit Macht Frei'. A man and a small girl walk through the gate as if they were headed on a jolly expedition. The blurb above distinctly states 'Children under 13 are not admitted'.

The second and equally startling picture for Western sensibilities is a portrait, captioned 'Cardinal at Auschwitz'. The Cardinal is Josef Cardinal Glemp, the head of the Catholic Church in Poland.

The brief entry devotes one long sentence to noting that the industrial town of Auschwitz, located between Krakow and Upper Silesia is of no interest to anyone; one short one to mentioning that Auschwitz is synonymous with 'the most horrific genocide in history'; and a complicated third one alerting us to the fact that in 1995, the fiftieth anniversary of the camp's liberation by the Russians was celebrated at the memorial in the grounds of Auschwitz 1, while four kilometres to the west at Birkenau or Auschwitz 2, there is a memorial to the '1.5 million people who died here as victims of the Nazi racist fanaticism'. Only towards the end of the second and last paragraph do we learn that over one million of these people were 'of Jewish origin'. (The figures, incidentally, are now generally agreed to be 1.6 million of whom ninety per cent were Jews.)

Apart from the ritual – though, in this case, deserved – genuflection to the liberating Russians, what is interesting about this entry is its evident unwillingness to acknowledge the association every Westerner instantly makes: Auschwitz is the place where over a million Jews were brutally exterminated. Rather, the internal assumption in this entry is that Auschwitz is a site of Polish memory, not specifically of Jewish memory. In the Polish national consciousness, Poles were the primary victims of the Nazis. Auschwitz, originally an internment camp for Polish political prisoners and eventually Russian POWs, is a place where Poles were martyred.

Poles, on the whole, do not understand how they, the victims of the Nazis, have come in the West to be associated with the killers. It was not Poles, after all, who dreamt up and operated the death camps. It was Germans. Then, too, the majority of Jews who were killed in the war were Polish Jews.

The statistics encourage this very Polish elision of Poles and Jews. Of some six million Jews who perished in the Holocaust, three million were Polish. Of the six million Polish nationals who died, three million were Jews and three million Christians.

Six million is the figure of Jewish deaths as it is of Polish deaths, including Polish Jews. In Polish eyes, the Poles' national suffering equals that of the Jews.

All of which goes a little way towards explaining the peculiar presence of the hardly philo-Semitic Cardinal Glemp in the tourist guide. Where there is true Polishness, particularly victimised Polishness, there must be Catholicism.

The Cardinal's presence has an additional factual link to Auschwitz on which the guide doesn't bother to comment – though an alert foreign visitor could not but fail to sense an anti-Semitic subtext. In 1984 Carmelite nuns established a convent at the perimeter fence of Auschwitz and constructed a twenty-four-foot wooden crucifix by its side. Protests from abroad were vociferous. Poles could not fathom them. Hadn't the Pope himself, back in 1971 when still a Cardinal, called for a church to be erected on this site, during a beatification ceremony in honour of Maximilian Kolbe, a rabidly anti-Semitic priest who died at Auschwitz after exchanging himself for a Polish prisoner? As blind to Jewish sensitivities as the majority of his countrymen and women, Wojtyla returned to Auschwitz eight years later, now as Pope, to name Auschwitz as the 'Golgotha of the contemporary world', thereby fusing the death of a martyred Christ with the mass murder of over a million Jews. Later, he chose to beatify Edith Stein, the Jewish convert to Catholicism killed in Auschwitz, who, in his words, 'died as a daughter of Israel for the glorification of the Holy name of God'.

In setting up their Auschwitz convent, the obedient Carmelite nuns were simply heeding their Pope. The neighbouring Poles were pleased. For them the cross was a sign of the redemption of the martyred dead. They could not see that for the Jews, it was symbol and signal of persecution, an affront to their murdered kin.

Controversy bubbled for years and boiled over in 1989 when an activist rabbi from New York and seven supporters scaled the convent walls, chanted prayers and read from the Torah. They were roughed up by Polish workmen who hurled anti-Semitic imprecations at them as well as paint, and evicted them. Cardinal Glemp chose this tense moment in Polish-Jewish relations to pronounce that a 'squad' of Jews had attempted to murder the nuns and that the Jewish-controlled world press would do better to call off its anti-Polish campaign.

I reflect on the muddy waters of Polish-Jewish relations as Monica and I cross into Warsaw's Grzybowski Square, location of one of the gates into the wartime ghetto. We are headed for a meeting in the new Jewish community centre in Twarda Street. Headed reluctantly. I am as sceptical of belief and believers as I am of any systems which assert single monolithic truths and their spokesmen. But here in Poland I am also curious. In this country of cemeteries, where no one knows exactly how many of Poland's three million Jews remain, there is a Jewish revival afoot. It seems to go hand in hand with the recent wave of anti-Semitism – as if grumbling, frozen spectres from the past have been resurrected with the lifting of the lid of Communist repression. Though this time the abstract anti-Semitism which needs no real Jews for objects has preceded the appearance of Jews themselves.

Recently, some five thousand of Poland's guesstimated 30,000 Jews have affiliated themselves to a practising Jewish community. They are mostly my generation or much younger. They study Torah and observe festivals and kosher rituals. Some are the products of adamantly secular families as uninterested in Jewishness as they were once interested in the Utopian promises of Communism. They have turned to Judaism because to embrace what the Communists persecuted and reviled can only be a good. Or they have chosen it because the anti-Semitic wave of the sixties made them realise that if you could be beaten up for being Jewish, Jewishness must matter. Some, who were close to the Solidarity underground, from 1985 on began surreptitiously to study Jewish texts and celebrate Jewish holidays together. Others have only recently discovered that a parent is Jewish – either because silence seemed the best course for the parent to take in overtly anti-Semitic times, or because death-bed confessions revealed wartime adoption from a fleeing Jew. Whatever the circumstances of discovery, they have, with the fall of Communism, chosen an orthodox Jewish identity. These are Jews who, unlike their grandparents, have been brought up thoroughly Polish, so they have no need to desire assimilation. Instead what they want is difference plus community within Poland. There is no talk of emigration to any of the old promised lands. Perhaps the phenomenon is not so very unlike American identity politics of recent years, with the caveat that Polish-Jewish roots are not elsewhere. These Jews want to be Jews and to belong in Poland.

We stand in front of the New Synagogue or Nozyk

Synagogue, founded in 1900. It is a solid, portly building of grey stone spread in a broad rectangle. Positioned in what was the Little Ghetto, it was saved from total destruction because the Nazis found it useful as a stable and fodder store. Hastily renovated after the war, and more thoroughly in the early eighties, it opened its doors again in 1983. Now these doors are charred and blackened, as is the hall. Earlier this year, the building was fire-bombed. No one was apprehended. *Plus ça change* . . .

But there is some change. The rabbi, who first arrived here as a student in the seventies, is American. His salary comes from the Ronald S. Lauder Foundation which also sponsors the Jewish Historical Institute and a host of more recent Jewish projects. That the Americans have bought into the free cultural as well as consumer market which the end of Communism created is hardly surprising. If the old Polish Jews went to America and brought a smattering of their origins with them, they have now come back to give the new Polish Jews a tinge of the American.

To the right of the synagogue, fronting a square filled with the bustle of coaches and tourists, is a broad arc of a building, painted in a white so sparkling one feels the Mediterranean has suddenly invaded Polish drizzle. This is the old congregation building, now home to a host of Jewish educational, social and cultural services. It is also the headquarters of *Midrasz*, a new journal of Jewish thought, launched in the spring of 1997. Its editor is Konstanty Gebert, a respected journalist whose reports from Bosnia won him international acclaim. It is Konstanty Gebert we are going to see.

He is a sturdy, vibrant man with a full biblical beard and a *yarmulke* perched on his curly hair. His handshake is firm, his English, American. He offers us good filter coffee at a corner table of an airy rectangle of an office. We talk a little about the magazine which contains a wide range of articles. There is a piece on Auschwitz and the politics of memory by Stanislaw Krajewski, a mathematician, who has become one of the leaders of the Polish-Jewish revival and who runs a Jewish identity hotline. There are commentaries on the Torah and on the basics of ceremonies, articles on Jewish artifacts and buildings abroad, as well as book reviews. Gebert's enthusiasm is contagious, yet part of me is uncomfortable with this championing of belief. Why revive what generations of European Jews sought to escape? It is as if these new Polish Jews are giving the Poles precisely what they want – traditional and recognisable Jews whom they can then proceed to fire-bomb.

But Gebert is an optimist. He tells us a strain of real philo-Semitism has arisen in Polish culture in the last twenty years. You can say 'fuck' and get no response. But the expletive 'Jew' makes people sit up. The Poles know that anti-Semitism is not legitimated by Europe, and certainly not by America. Then, too, in a mono-ethnic country, Jews are interesting, morally and intellectually.

As for Polish anti-Semitism, it has always existed, but it was the Nazis who strengthened it and gave it legitimacy. At the beginning of the war, even the most rabid of anti-Semitic cardinals defended individual Jews and stopped at murder. Then the Poles saw that the heavens didn't darken at Nazi brutality; nor did the Allies bomb anyone for the sake of Jews. So anti-

Semitism was strengthened by the war. Now, with Europe, things can go the other way.

Perhaps Gebert is right. Here and there around Poland, small towns are renewing their interest in their buried Jewish pasts. Archives are being formed. Plaques are going up on buildings. Cemeteries are being reconstituted. Whether this is an effect of the lucrative Holocaust-tourism industry – which brings three-quarters of a million people to Auschwitz and 300,000 to Maidanek each year – or whether it marks a real shift in Polish-Jewish relations, only time will tell.

As we go out into the busy square, I hear a young man's vivid laugh. He is talking to an Israeli tourist and he says in response to some query, 'My mother always says she has one Jewish son and one Christian son. That's the way it is.'

If that's the way it is and it can produce laughter, maybe we've reached the best point yet in this half century's relations between Poles and Jews.

In the desert of stone which was all that remained of the teeming Warsaw Ghetto after the war, the first memorial to the dead was a small block of red sandstone. Its round surface plate is slightly tilted towards what was once the ghetto gate which Nazi tanks tried to storm in order to quell the unexpected uprising of Jewish warriors on April 19, 1943. Raised three years to the day after this event, the monument reads: 'In memory of those who died in unparalleled and heroic struggle for the dignity and freedom of the Jewish nation, for Free Poland and for the Liberation of Man.'

The text is from all accounts a true representation of what the idealistic young fighters of the ghetto sought when they pitted their desperate will and makeshift arms against the military might of the Nazis. But in its linking of a Free Poland with a free Jewish nation, the inscription may seem a little odd to today's Western visitors, whom a half century of shifting Holocaust memory has hardly prepared for a fusion of aims between Poles and Jews. Written into the Jewish Holocaust story as enemies, the Poles were also for years largely deprived of any narrative or monuments which commemorated their own heroism – their resistance and uprising against the Nazis. A story of brave, independent Poles, struggling against the Nazis for the freedom of their nation through an underground linked to an exile government in London, did not suit Communist politics, which preferred an account where the Russians were forefronted as the great liberators. In one of those mordant ironies of twentieth-century history, the Poles, in order collectively to remember their own wartime heroism, had sometimes to remember themselves through the Warsaw Ghetto Jews.

We stand in the windblown square dominated by Nathan Rapoport's impressive Warsaw Ghetto monument, dedicated on April 19, 1948 before some twenty thousand spectators. Now the square is bordered by the nondescript apartment blocks of Zamenhofa Street. At the time, the monument was the only structure in a wasteland which stretched for miles. Its massive hewn stone wall rose from the debris like a monolithic tombstone, echoing not only the ghetto wall, but also the Western Wall in Jerusalem. Locally, the monument is known as the Memorial to the Ghetto Heroes.

Andrzej Latko is with us. He seems altogether at his ease in front of this supposedly Jewish memorial, and enjoins us to look at all sides of the massive tombstone. At the front, a group of giant sculpted figures struggles to get free from the prison of the wall. These are worker heroes, at once Jewish and prole-tarian. Dressed in tatters, vulnerably exposed, each grasps a weapon. The leader, Anielewicz, classically bare-breasted, clutches a grenade and strides forward, leading his people out of the confines of the wall into freedom. On the reverse side, a bas-relief depicts the other aspect of ghetto experience – the martyrs, a long timeless line of suffering humanity. The old and the frail clutch at each other and at their children. A Torah scroll is held aloft, but the people are bent by the weight of the wall.

At Israel's Yad Vashem Holocaust Museum this movement between the old and the new which the two sides of the wall represent is made even clearer. The ghetto monument was reproduced there in 1968 when there were fears that the Communist unleashing of a new wave of anti-Semitism in Poland might result in its destruction. In Yad Vashem the back and front of the ghetto monument stand side by side so one can read them as a narrative of progress, the old martyrs giving way to the new heroic fighters. In the founding myth of Israel, the Holocaust is triumphantly redeemed in the bold struggle to establish the new state.

I am not a good visitor of memorials. Nietzsche's line about monuments being petrified history always comes back to me. I find myself more interested in the formal and aesthetic properties of Rapoport's art than in the remembering of the ghetto the monument bids me to engage in. The only remembering that comes to me is the memory of having read that the granite blocks of this monumental wall had originally been set aside by the Nazi sculptor, Arno Breker, for Hitler's victory monument in Berlin. Fortunately, history caught him out. Rapoport found the blocks neatly stacked, still awaiting delivery, in a Swedish quarry in 1947 and had them shipped to Warsaw.

Monica seems to feel much as I do. She tells me that in their cellar in Connecticut, they have a giant head of her father, sculpted by Nathan Rapoport. They don't know what to do with it. The head is so big, so domineering.

Andrzej is patently the only one of us who doesn't feel he is in the midst either of art or of petrified history. He tells us that throughout the eighties, Solidarity would lay a wreath here on April 19 to commemorate a heroic liberation struggle and as a sign of their own resistance to the Communist regime. In the 1988 commemoration, then Solidarity leader, Lech Walesa, declared the uprising of the Jewish fighters to be the most Polish of all uprisings – one which was soon to be re-enacted in another Gdansk shipyard strike.

It was also in 1988 that the government, perhaps partly in an effort to defuse the wider revolutionary potential of the monument and reinscribe it safely in history, created a Memory Lane. Through a series of black syenite slabs, this links the monument to the Ghetto Uprising, to the Umschlagsplatz – the site from which the ghetto Jews were deported to Treblinka. Each point on the Memory Lane tells part of the ghetto story and evokes key names: Janusz Korczak, indefatigable champion of the ghetto's orphans, the poet Itzhak Katzenelson, the archivist and historian Emmanuel Ringelblum, amongst them. On the site of the Mila 18 bunker, there is a funeral mound several feet high, as high as the level of rubble from the destruction of the ghetto originally rose. It was here that Anielewicz, his wife and several other ghetto fighters, surrounded on all sides by the Nazis and choking on the gas bombs which had been hurled into the bunker, at last took their own lives on May 8, 1943. The few who escaped joined the people's resistance army, the Gwardia Ludowa, and died later in the partisan struggle.

For a reason I cannot explain, it is only when we reach the Umschlagsplatz that the full weight of this terrible history bears down on my shoulders. Stawki Street is a wide boulevard. Traffic belts along its arrow-straight expanse. We stand within a broken geometry of luminous white marble rising to the height of the ghetto wall. Through the openings in these walls, we can see the building which housed the SS command in charge of deportations as well as the hospital turned prison where the victims awaiting the fatal trains to Treblinka were crammed. It is on this very spot that Korczak stood with his orphan children, that my paternal family stood, the pistol-happy SS guards herding them, shouting, shoving them on to the trains of extinction ... During nine weeks in the summer of 1942, five to six thousand people a day were crushed into freight cars here to be transported to that fatal destination where up to 15,000 were gassed each day. I can smell their bewilderment, their fear, the rank odour of bodies crushed together in terror and heat.

Like a ritual prayer shawl, the new monument's cool white wreathes round us with a horizontal band of black. Names glimmer on the white surface in the growing dusk. Not family names, but first names – Chaim, Ester, Mordechai – the names mothers use, the first names European Jews give to their offspring, in that traditional commemoration of the dead which is the act of naming.

Wartime: 1941–43

My imagination refuses to conjure up the repetitive dailiness of life in the Warsaw Ghetto. The end blots out everything that came before. All I can see is this end – the trains bound for the gas chambers of Treblinka. My paternal aunts were there and my uncles; perhaps too, my grandfather Reuben, though it may be that he died earlier in the typhoid epidemic that raged through the ghetto in the cusp of that year. We cannot know. Some 850,000 Jews from all corners of Europe were murdered at Treblinka. There are no records for all these deaths. In the autumn of 1943, when the Treblinka killings ended, the bodies were dug up and burned on orders from Berlin. Camp buildings were razed and the ground planted over with trees. The Nazis wanted all memory of the Jews and of their own acts of atrocity extinguished.

All this, the tragedy, I can almost imagine. But somehow, the atmosphere of life in the ghetto remains opaque. The long, arduous, extended everydayness of it is the problem – as it must have been a millionfold for its inhabitants. All I can begin to compare it to is life in a prison. It is a prison in which the

guards' random acts of sadism are sanctioned, indeed encouraged, by policy. It is a prison in which the inmates have committed no crime except that of having been born. They do
not know they are in prison: after all, they have not been tried.
Nor do they know that all sentences here carry the death
penalty. Their innocence, their vulnerability frightens me.

None of us can work out exactly how long my father spent
in the ghetto. Nor do we know whether he was transported
from the labour camp in Pruszków or fled to the ghetto in
search of family and what he thought might be sanctuary. The
dates seem to mean nothing to my mother. Aron was away and
then he was back. He himself rarely spoke about it. Probably
he was in the ghetto from February 1941 until that summer.
There survives a photograph he had of a woman in a summery
cotton frock stretched out on the ground. Her eyes are huge in
her skeletal face. She is too weak to move, starving. My father
would look at this photograph from time to time. He never
said who the woman was. Perhaps he didn't know. She was,
simply, 'the ghetto'.

The ghetto then was deprivation, the silent daily suffering
of the weak – women, children, the old and frail. It was also
degradation – the inevitable dehumanising that comes from
living in a brutal, desperate world where death is everywhere
and often casual. Yes, there were a score of underground newspapers, occasional and illicit art exhibits, secret schools and
Zionist and Bundist gatherings. Yes, there were family and
friends and local housing committees organised to help the
poorest. But there was also forced daily labour, often under the
eagle eye and quick whip of Gestapo officers. Without work,

there were no ration cards. Then too, there were Jewish police and Polish police. No one ever walked through the streets at a normal pace. Everyone ran. There was bribery at every level to obtain the most basic of necessities. At risk of imprisonment or death, children and women jumped over or crawled through holes in the wall in a daily search for food, gave it to their families or sold it to the highest bidder.

Why didn't Aron and his family, the beloved elder sisters whom he respected almost as mothers, make their escape at the first opportunity? They had the wealth necessary for bribery. They had the potential help of brother-in-law, Adek. As a teenager, I used to press my father on this point. I was full of hostility for this blind Jewish passivity. Aron would shrug, mumble something about the fact that no one knew they were all to die. There was no precedent for this particular atrocity. Or he would quote the stubborn old patriarch who was his father, 'We have to stay amongst our own. There's no other way. And money will provide. It always has.'

Aron's voice, when he cited his father, had a touch of youthful bitterness, as if he were still caught up in the battle between the generations which so acutely demarcated the attitudes of young from old during the war.

Once he said to me, 'Imagine you're in the local train station and a voice comes over the megaphone and says "all passengers to platform one". Even if the trains haven't been running on time, even if you're fed up with the railway authorities, you go, don't you? You're conditioned to trust that megaphone voice, to follow its orders.' Trust, even an unwilling, sceptical trust, is the fabric of society. And the Polish Jews, many of whom had in any case for generations lived in Jewish quarters, had little choice but to make the best they could of the rule of the ghetto.

Aron didn't for long. Despite his uncertainty about his ability to survive disguised as a Pole, he made his bid for a haphazard freedom beyond the walls. This must have been before November 1941 when the death penalty for leaving the ghetto was instituted. In that month, the first public executions of captured Jewish escapees were held in front of the prison on Gesia Street. By the horrified Jews of the ghetto, these were known as executions for 'crossing the street' – streets they had crossed all their lives. As my father always admitted with a touch of shame, he wasn't a particularly brave man and he might have been deterred from his walk to freedom if he had known of the immediate consequences.

So Aron made his way out of the ghetto. Possibly he bribed the Polish work-team police and slipped away, while they were looking in the opposite direction, once the work brigade was across the ghetto gate. Or more probably, as my brother claims, Uncle Adek performed one of his miracles, strutted up to an SS man, flashed a document and ordered, '*Geben Sie mir dieser verflüchter Jude.*' 'Give me that damn Jew, over there.'

In either case, my father arrived in Adek's house on Czerniakowska Street. Here he was promptly told by his brother-in-law that he would have to go straight into hiding. There was no way in his present state that he could pass as an Aryan. Whatever his *Kennkarte* might say, his eyes betrayed him. Their haunted melancholy, that hunted look of fear, would immediately give him away as a Jew.

It was no simple business posing as a Gentile in a world of well-paid informers and blackmailers, who scoured streets and railway stations in search of potentially lucrative Jews. Germans could usually be duped. Since their Jewish population before the war had been less than two per cent, their Jews were largely imaginary. Poles, however, could tell the real thing. Never mind the superficial characteristics of face and colouring and clothes. They could also recognise accents and above all, they could recognise the look. Aron had to change his demeanour and his deportment and his mannerisms. He had to appear assured, fearless. There could be no glancing over his shoulder, no swift give-away movements of the eyes. He had to be lively and cheerful, at ease. Then, too, he needed to perfect his knowledge of Catholicism, learn his catechism and his prayers and his saints' days. All this he would accomplish while he remained in the cosmetic firm's warehouse.

Aron went into hiding. He practised. He also grew a Hitler moustache and parted his hair along Führer lines. By the New Year, he was as ready as he would ever be to go out into the world of Gentiles. He had a new name too. He was Kazimierz Kowalski (Kajik for short), with a list of forebears and baptismal priests and family occupations that had to be rattled off by rote to any interrogator.

Meanwhile, my mother had come back to Warsaw with Staszek and Sara. For a brief time the three of them stayed with Adek. It was Adek who with his characteristic devil-may-care boldness gave my brother toy pistols and taught him to go 'bang, bang' at passing German officers.

This frightened my mother, who was coaching him to be a good little boy, one who said his nightly prayers in front of the crucifix which hung over his bed; one who never pulled his trousers down when anyone was looking or ever peed before strangers' eyes. He was, after all, circumcised, though this was not the reason given to Staszek. It was simply good manners. Staszek had to learn a grim form of self-control, particularly during journeys about town.

Her son's behaviour apart, Hena was fearless. She always travelled in the front – the German – section of trolleys and buses. Germans, on the whole, could be counted on to be polite to attractive, well-dressed young women and their children. Then too, in the front section, there was less likelihood of bumping into give-away Polish acquaintances who might blurt out the wrong name; or of being asked for one's papers.

Since living with Adek in the longer term would inevitably create suspicion, Hena found a flat for her now reunited family. My father's presence was a problem. Not only was his Polish second-skin still a somewhat ungainly fit, but young male Poles had to be gainfully employed and carry work-cards. Aron had neither employment, nor a card. Yet Hena couldn't bear the thought of them being separated again and in her new dominant mode, she was trebly certain only she could protect him. The result was a bizarre living arrangement. In the new flat, Aron posed as a tenant, Sara, who still insisted on lighting Sabbath candles, as a maid, while my mother was a young woman whose husband had been taken off to work in Germany.

To make this charade, in which the forfeit was death, convincing, was not easy. In the generalised atmosphere of fear,

Polish neighbours could easily turn informers. The matter of native anti-Semitism apart, they stood to gain by exposing Jews or to lose by sheltering them. By October 1942, the penalty for helping Jews was execution. The fact that the Nazis found it necessary to impose the death penalty in Poland and in no other occupied country suggests, against all popularly received wisdom, that the Poles were rather more prone than other nations to helping the Jews.

Every morning my father would leave his lodgings punctually, a lunch bag in hand, as if he were going off to work. In fact he was headed for the streets. He would roam them for hours and then trudge home at five o'clock, his shift over. Sometimes, he would go to the cinema and watch German propaganda films or sit in one of the out-of-the-way cafés which had sprung up in convents or houses as people turned their hands to any available form of subsistence. And he would read. He read anything he could lay his hands on. In these months he remembered reading Schopenhauer and Nietzsche. Occasionally, he would sit in a church, rest his feet, bend his head in prayer.

All of this on the surface seems pleasant enough. In fact, the streets were treacherous. The Germans conducted frequent impromptu checks during any of which one was likely to be arrested. There were also the notorious *lapanki*, the brutal round-ups in which whole blocks were cordoned off by armed SS and all able-bodied individuals promptly shipped off to labour camps in Germany. Any protest met the muzzle of a gun. These *lapanki* increased dramatically as the Nazi campaign in Russia swallowed up young Germans and left less and less native labour available.

Like a wanted man, Aron had to maintain a constant vigilance. He was ever alert to the changing pattern of pedestrians on a street, to the varying sounds of footsteps behind him, to the eyes about him. A suspicious glance could denote a perfidious *szmalcownik*, a blackmailer. The presence of Polish policemen, who it was said could smell Jews, would set him off in a new direction. A whole geography of evasion became familiar to him – a network of lanes and alleys and courtyards which abutted on new lanes. It was better not to leap on to trolleys since a check on one of these allowed no escape. So he walked, walked quickly and purposefully, pretending to have a destination other than the five o'clock one which would at last lead him home.

This went on for almost a year. Sometime towards the end of 1942, my mother who always kept up cheerful and chatty relations with the neighbours, was told tearfully by one of them that her husband had been taken off by the Gestapo for interrogation. My mother shivered in apprehension as she consoled her neighbour. Was the woman telling her this because she suspected something about her tenant, Pan Kowalski? Everyone knew that behind the stone walls of the Pawiak prison hideous torture was carried out with the goal of extracting information – about runaway Jews, about the underground.

Three days after his arrest, the neighbour came home. His hair had turned white. His toe- and fingernails had been extracted. He had been savagely beaten. Each beating had been attended with questions about the whereabouts of Jews.

This incident coincided with the October 1942 ruling which put the death penalty in place for any Pole harbouring Jews. In one of those quick, instinctual decisions which became her trademark, my mother determined that it was time to sever relations with her brother and to acquire a new identity and new address. The fact that the families knew each other's whereabouts made each potentially treacherous to the other. Who could guess what Aron or she might divulge under torture? The small tight unit of the immediate family had to stay together, but there was no point endangering anyone else.

With a careless bravura akin to her brother's, Hena marched into the Warsaw Town Hall and asked to see the supervisor in charge of registrations. Something in her demeanour and her insistence that she needed to speak to the chief privately must have seen her past secretaries and assistants, for she was asked to wait and eventually ushered through to the head man. In retrospect, she imagines they must have thought she was either a madwoman or a mistress.

'I need to speak to you personally,' she told the man. 'It's urgent.'

Perhaps he was curious. Perhaps he liked her looks. In any event, the man told her to wait for him in a nearby café.

When he came to join her, she had her story ready. She told him she had just arrived in Warsaw from the countryside. Her family was dead. Her husband had been taken off to Germany. She had a small child and she desperately needed work. In order to work, of course, she needed a registered-in-Warsaw identity which she didn't have.

The man considered her. 'You're very young and very brave. I could arrest you right now, you know.'

Hena nodded. 'But when you're drowning, you clutch at

straws to help yourself. You're my straw. You can kill me. Or you can help me.'

The man laughed. He laughed and laughed.

'I'll help you, because I'm afraid for you, because you're recklessly brave.'

This is how my mother recounts the episode. When pressed on why she confided in this particular man, she always responds that he had a good face. 'I know faces. I really do,' she repeats over and over, even now that her judgement has lost its sure touch. About Mieczyslaw Oselinski she was certainly right. He did help. He helped a great deal. He gave her his private telephone line and told her to ring him in two days' time. By then, he had a set of papers for her and a Warsaw registration.

He also eventually provided her with a double set of ration coupons – coupons which were only available to registered workers – which she sold or traded to supplement other needs. Her new Warsawian name was Hania Sawicka.

Hania Sawicka found a flat in Zoliborz, a pleasant and respectable suburb of Warsaw where the majority of the population were white-collar workers, civil servants and professionals. In their new home, she told her son he had a new name. He was now Staszek Sawicki. Staszek looked up at her with a three-year-old's righteous indignation. She had told him never to lie and now she wanted him to lie. Yes, she said. Only in this instance. When people came up to him in the street and told him what a sweet and pretty boy he was and asked him his name, as they so often did, he was now to reply, 'Stanislaw Sawicki'. Staszek was not a particularly obedient child. But in this respect, he complied with Hania's orders. This is something my mother has never ceased to marvel at: their lives were at the precarious mercy of a temperamental toddler, yet miraculously they were safe.

Over the years, Staszek grew adept at the various masquerades which were his existence. He knew that his father was and wasn't quite his father and he was never to call him 'Tatus' when a stranger was present. He knew his grandmother was his 'babka' and was also a maid or a visitor. He knew that he must never speak of his Uncle Adek in public. In that tense symbiosis which characterised his relations with his mother, he took his unspoken signals from her. Only once did he betray her. But that came later.

Other changes followed close on the heels of Staszek's new name and address. His mother now went out to work every day. Pan Oselinski had found her a post at the City Hall in the work registration bureau, the Arbeitsamt. Staszek didn't like this. He was furious at the forced separation from his mother. One day when they were out in the streets, he flung a stone at a passing German and went 'bang bang' with his pistol just as he had been shown to do by his beloved Uncle Adek, whom he never saw any more. His mother rushed him home, told him he must never do that again. It was wrong. Very wrong. God would punish him. 'Which God?' railed an angry Staszek. Not this one here above the bed. Why, he could take him in his hands and break him into a hundred pieces. And he proceeded to fling the crucifix on the floor.

Hania chided and calmed him. But she was at her wits' end.

Staszek was most disobedient when it came to matters of religion. He had unconsciously picked up the family cues. Perhaps he sensed his father's secret pride in his rebellion against prayers and catechism. None the less, if Staszek were to draw attention to them before they had succeeded in getting new papers for Aron and her mother, the results would be dire. Hania went to see Oselinski. He had become a good friend and all her instincts told her she could confide in him, despite the dangerous nature of the information she was about to impart. She said to Oselinski that she hadn't told him the whole truth. Her husband had come back. And her mother was here, too. No, she wasn't dead.

'I would like you to meet them,' Hania rushed on before the frown on Oselinski's face could find words. 'I need to get papers for them.'

There must have been something in her desperation, her innocent trust, which moved Oselinski. He came to the house. Hania didn't need to say it aloud. One look at Aron and he knew the rest of the truth. Jews. 'But not you?' he asked her.

She nodded.

Oselinski stared at her in disbelief. After a moment, he shrugged. He was a man of honour. He looked from Aron to Sara and back again. 'Your mother will pass. We'll find her a job. But your husband ... The best solution would be for him to go to Germany where they think they've already mopped up all the Jews. You'll be better off separated.'

Aron was more than prepared to go. He didn't want his Jewish appearance to endanger his family any longer. Nor could he bear to sit passively by and watch the shrinking of the ghetto area. It could mean only one thing. Death. Death and more death. He needed to move, to engage in something. But Hania was adamant. If Aron left, her life would be one perpetual anxiety about him. She couldn't bear the thought of that. They must all stay together.

Within a few weeks, Oselinski came up with the appropriate forged documents. Aron was now Pan Zabłocki. For Sara, there was a job as a maid to a German doctor, a woman who lived in the best part of Warsaw and had a room for her to go along with the job. Paradoxically, the German quarter was the safest place to be. Few checks were carried out there. For little Staszek, while Hania went out to work, there was now a minder, an elderly French spinster, whom the war had trapped in Poland. Hania reissued the command that he must be a polite boy and never take his trousers down in front of the new nanny.

The months rolled on. Aron – ever vigilant – walked the streets. As he built up more courage in his Aryan identity, he arranged for the occasional foray into Pruszków to retrieve, piecemeal, the stored textiles which would augment their resources. Once he made the journey himself. This was precarious and unwise. Neighbours recognised him and their silence could not be relied on, even for money. On subsequent occasions he arranged for an intermediary, a woman, to act as his agent. The woman collected the goods, then she or Hania went out to sell the fabric to Warsaw shops. Hania also carried on with her job. On the occasional weekend, her mother would come to visit.

One day the landlord of the Zoliborz house, a *Volksdeutsche*, with whom Hania maintained cordial relations, stopped her on the landing, ushered her into his apartment and told her that she should be wary of her French nanny.

'Why?' Hania asked, all innocence. She was already wary of everyone, particularly of neighbours who gossiped and tattled.

The man cleared his throat. 'She's found you out. Your tenant ... your husband ... she suspects he's a Jew.'

'Silly woman!' Hania laughed. 'You know these old spinsters. Always imagining things.'

The man took hold of her wrist. He gave her a meaningful look. 'None the less, you should get rid of her.'

'When I've found someone to replace her.'

Hania breezed away, only instantly to ring Oselinski. Oselinski said he would engage the woman in his own service and keep an eye on her for the time that it took Hania to find secure new lodgings.

It took some two months.

The exact nature of my mother's relations with Oselinski remains mysterious. Were his brave and generous acts a form of inducement or payment for sexual favours? Was he, in other words, a lover, as my brother has always suspected, perhaps picking up clues from the atmosphere of the time? In staunch maternal fashion my mother has always denied this, simply saying that Oselinski was a fine and honourable man. Cynicism about wartime relations coupled with her persistent aura of sexual adventure is what induces the speculation. Most days, I take her at her word. My sense of her is that she far prefers to flirt and seduce than to be free with her favours. But then, I am a daughter.

Whatever the floating truth, Oselinski emerges as a brave and good man.

During one of the last conversations Hania held with the *Volksdeutsche* landlord who had been so kind to her, they stood on a balcony of the Zoliborz house and watched the distance fill with clouds of smoke. Overhead the Stukas circled and swooped, raining fire. It was May 1943. The ghetto was burning.

On the nineteenth day of the previous month, the first day of Passover, some fifteen hundred youths, armed with home-made Molotov cocktails and an assortment of pistols and sticks and stones, had begun an heroic last-ditch stand against the Nazi enemy in the name of Jewish honour and a Jewish future. Himmler had chosen Passover, which that year coincided with Easter, for the final liquidation of the ghetto: the date not only evoked traditional blood libels and Eastern European pogroms, but had the advantage of providing a birthday present for his Führer. Against all odds and with some help from the Polish Resistance, the ghetto warriors held out for six weeks. The cost in lives was terrible. Amidst the devastation, General Jürgen Stroop, Commander of the Nazi forces, could report that 56,065 Jews had been apprehended, while 19,929 had died in the struggle. How accurate these figures are is unclear, but only a few Jews remained alive to join the partisans in the woods or find shelter on the Aryan side. Of the ghetto itself, all that remained was rubble and charred earth which the forced labour squads flattened into an empty expanse of wasteland.

As the smoke billowed, my mother's landlord smiled with a

touch of pride. 'Amazing. What the Poles couldn't accomplish for so many years, Hitler has arranged quickly and magnificently. The end of the Jews in Poland.'

'Let's see what he arranges next for the rest of us,' my mother murmured and after a calculated moment turned on her well-polished heels.

On Site

As if stubbornly to counter the logic of statistics, Monica still has family in Poland. There are cousins and their children and more cousins, all linked through a grandparental generation of three siblings.

I walk down the curving staircase of the Hotel Europejski to meet Monica and the first of these cousins. They are sitting face to face on one of the lobby's vast sofas. Both of them are in tears. They wipe them away hastily as I approach and cousin Joasia gives me a shy smile. She is a small dark woman with a gnomish face, lively dark eyes and a snub of a nose. A writer and dramaturge, she lives in Krakow, where for many years she ran the famous artists' cellar there – a kind of literary café-cum-cabaret, set in one of the small side streets which lead off the beautiful church square.

Spread on the coffee table in front of them are sheets of paper. They contain a sprawling family tree, its roots stretching back to an early nineteenth-century Frankfurt rabbi who performed a miracle that became legend by purportedly expanding the street beneath his window to prevent a collision between two oncoming carriages. Joasia loves the miracle. Her eyes grow wide as she recounts it. It is not the miracle which has produced the tears. These come from more recent history.

Everyone, it seems, is engaged in memory work. Recently Joasia decided to write a book about her family's past and began the business of excavating a genealogy. She has tracked and traced, unearthed letters and writings. Only one chapter remains opaque – the one about her own wartime childhood. It is a period of deep amnesia: when asked to talk about it, there is only blankness and tears.

At the start of the war, three women made up her nearest family – her powerful and domineering grandmother, her mother and herself. When the bombs began to drop on Warsaw, the three escaped to the capacious house of a well-known writer who lived in the countryside around Pruszków. When their presence here grew dangerous, Joasia remembers fleeing by night through fields and forest and finally, in exhaustion, knocking at the door of a small peasant house. They were invited in by kindly strangers and in a piece of utter good fortune, the single night's stay turned into three months. After they had to leave, her mother placed Joasia in a convent in Warsaw, which eventually was moved into the countryside. For over three years, from the age of seven to ten, Joasia didn't see her mother. It is those years that are lost in amnesia. Like a wound overlaid with scar tissue so thick it has displaced the memory of the original injury, Joasia can only cry when the scar is scratched. For years, she didn't even look at it, obliterated its existence. Only recently has she begun to pick at it. But even now, she cannot bring herself to meet the son of the peasants who sheltered them and who has been in touch with her. Nor can she confront the possibility of returning to the convent to visit the nuns, one or two of whom, she has been told, remember her.

We force ourselves out of the swoon of story and go for a stroll through Warsaw's old city centre, replicated in exact detail in an admirable feat of post-war reconstruction. Elegant eighteenth-century terraces of pale pink and green and ochre cluster around the expanse of the main square where café parasols billow an invitation. It is only as we walk that the resemblance between Monica and her cousin strikes me. It manifests itself not so much in raven hair or disposition of feature, but in the walk itself, an amble of kinship.

In a moment of nostalgia for the rites of tourism we haven't been enacting, we drop into a graceful church on a side street. No sooner have we crossed the threshold, than Joasia crosses herself with the speed of long-learned gesture. This instant and automatic genuflection takes me by surprise. A moment ago, she had been saying that her daughter, like so many of her generation a radical during the years of martial law in the early eighties, had recently manifested an interest in her Jewishness – a Jewishness which has only and ever been a fact of birth to Joasia. Mother and daughter had even both laughed and decided that Jews make the best husbands – something which, given the fact that both had had German first husbands, could only be hearsay. Yet Joasia kneels and crosses herself in church. Whatever it is she has blocked out about her war years in the convent, something has evidently remained. In that game of chance and possibilities which one plays with oneself when

revisiting sites of family life, I find myself wondering whether
my brother would cross himself like that had destinies turned
out differently.

Later we meet a younger member of Monica's family. There
is a familiar air about him. He is the kind of Central European
intellectual I was once taught by – a mixture of cuddly warmth
and analytic intelligence. And indeed, Marek lectures at the
University of Warsaw, as well as writing a column for the main
Warsaw newspaper. As we walk and chat about the poor turn-
out in the national elections, Marek notes that what Poland
needs, far more than politics now, is to build up the institutions
of civil society. Basic, everyday democracy has been lacking
since '48, perhaps before. Everyone still has a tendency to
depend on the long arm of the State for change.

I ask him whether the Jewish revival in Poland may in some
way also be part of a hunger for an open society whose institutions are independent of the State. He shrugs. He is Jewish,
of course, but not particularly interested in Jewishness. I find
myself relieved to learn that this possibility is still open to Poles
raised after the war. One can still be invisibly Jewish and yet
not need to hide the fact.

Marek mentions his university department's connection
with the ENA (Ecole Nationale d'Administration) in Paris and
how very much it helps young Poles to have contact with life
in Western democracies. He himself spent some time in Paris –
after a few months of incarceration during the '81–'83 period
of martial rule imposed in an attempt to break popular support
for Solidarnosz. As we talk about his Paris days, during which
he did research and wrote on the evolution of the Committee

for Cultural Freedom, I suddenly have one of those 'small world' moments. I have read his unpublished manuscript. Circuitously it found its way into my hands when I was researching my East–West novel, *The Things We Do for Love*. We all laugh and talk late into the night. At one point it emerges that Marek's present preoccupations are with the politics of memory. What else!

As we approach the millennium, it seems we are all preoccupied by memory. To construct a future, we need to unearth new narratives of the past. Pasts which have been buried by repressive regimes and left to fester or pasts transformed by Cold War politics; or simply pasts relegated to the limbo of latency because they were too painful to think about.

Another dank grey day. Spruce and punctual, Andrzej Latko comes to fetch us in his little Polish Fiat. It is the same car he drove me in ten years ago. It still runs, its gears creaking with age as he manoeuvres it through the dense traffic of a Warsaw morning. We cut across to the long steep road which winds down from the Barbican to the Vistula and judder along the riverside thoroughfare. Some forty minutes of Soviet-style tower-blocks and rather more attractive post-Soviet residential developments later and we turn off the main road into a leafy enclave of cobbled streets, lantern lamps and family houses, intermingled with small thirties apartment buildings. Andrzej pulls up in front of one of these: a square three-storey structure, from which the grey casing of concrete has dropped off here and there to reveal large patches of brown brick. A wire-mesh fence surrounds the building. Shrubs poke through its grille-work. Under the slab of a porch covering, a number plate boldly announces, Ul. Zielona 44.

Andrzej smiles at me, waiting for a response. This is the house in which he and his father shared an apartment with my mother and brother in the months leading up to the Warsaw Uprising. He points me to two side windows, overlooking a side and back garden. These, he tells me proudly, were my mother's. I shake away the scales of Western prejudice and try to see the building through his eyes, my mother's eyes when she first came here. It must have felt new in the war years, new and comfortable and functional – a suburban haven of private toilets and working water pipes and greenery. The greenery is even in the street's name. Behind the house, during the war, there were only fields and the garden.

'That was our life source,' Andrzej says, 'a ready plot of potatoes and cabbages, a bulwark against hunger. We never went very hungry.' He gives me his grin again. There is an enthusiasm about him which I can't replicate. I realise that he is excited to be here. He is young again here and not only young, but someone who has overcome, who has survived. Survived to come back here with the daughter of a woman who once saved his life.

He taps me on the shoulder and points to one of the larger brick-exposed areas near the top of the building. 'That's what one of the bomb blasts did. It's never been repaired. And over there,' he taps me again, 'that's where I saw an SS man kill a neighbour, a partisan I think he was. I was terrified. We were all terrified. They used to burst into houses and make such a racket. And that new house over there, that's where one of the bombs fell.' He claps his hands together as if smashing a fly. 'Come.'

I look up and down the leafy street and shiver. Everything is shrouded in a sudden uncanny quiet.

'My old school is gone,' Andrzej says as we pile into the car. We drive for a few minutes through the tree-lined streets. 'But this, this is still here.'

We walk down a small slope and abruptly, we come upon a glimmering lake. Bushy trees are mirrored in its still depths. Perched on a rock, a boy casts a fishing line into the water.

'This is where Pan Kazik, your father, taught me to swim. He just threw me in.'

'He did that to me, too.'

'It works.'

We smile in odd complicity.

When we turn, I notice that the jagged boulder behind us has a plaque fixed to its centre.

'Someone died here,' Andrzej explains.

'In the bombing?' Monica asks.

'No, no. He drowned. A peace-time death.' Andrzej gives us his wry smile.

The streets behind us bore no commemorative plaques. The war dead are too numerous to have their individuality publicly remembered.

We drive on, a kilometre or two, across the main thorough-fare and park. We are in what looks like an English common. A Great Dane lopes across the grass. Two youths sprint along-side a mastiff. We make our way in the opposite direction towards a wooded stream. On its other side stands a vast red-brick structure. There are machine guns perched on its roof and at its side, a team of old military vehicles, their numbers still clearly visible on their tank-like rear doors. This is the old Fortress of Sadyba, built by Pilsudski in the great days of Poland's heroism. After the evacuation of Warsaw, it was the site where thousands were herded, a stopping point into the unknown.

'This is where my father and I came,' Andrzej says. 'We spent three days here without food. He was intended for Germany, but he spoke the language and overheard what his fate was to be. So when the trains they piled us on to chugged along, we managed to jump off in the midst of a meadow in the countryside. Somehow we got by until it was over.'

On the way back into the city centre, I ask Andrzej how he feels now when he sees so many German tourists and businessmen in the streets of Warsaw. He gives us his characteristic shrug and in his tactful way, says, 'No. It's fine. It's good for the country.'

I press him. 'So you hold no grudges?'

The shrug again. 'If we were to hold grudges ... where would we be? It's only when they complain about how things are or start giving orders, then ... But look, we're at the Lazienki Park, the most beautiful place in Warsaw.'

Andrzej tells us how during the war, this park, effectively the grounds of the last Polish king's summer residence, was closed to Poles, as were all the streets bordering it. This grandest part of the city, with its stately homes, now mostly embassies, became the German sector. In front of one of these elegant houses, Polish partisans assassinated the head of the Gestapo in 1944, provoking appalling mass reprisals.

We stop and walk along past embassies, towards a mammoth art deco building. Atop its towering, colonnaded portico, the Polish eagle spreads its wings. To the right is a small sign, announcing the Ministry of the Interior. Through the wrought-iron grate, we see an internal courtyard around which the building shapes a looming square. Nothing stirs. This was once the inner sanctum of Nazi power, headquarters of the Gestapo, the building euphemistically known by the name of the street on which it stands, Aleje Szuhca – as if the function it contained was too terrible to speak. Behind these windows, below this paving, hideous torture was enacted.

I touch the ridge of the columns, feel the coldness of stone. Here is the original site of my father's recurring nightmares, the location of his final delirium. Do I want to will this mute stone into speech?

Wartime: 1943–45

It was a bright day early in June of 1943. With the razing of the ghetto, the shape of Warsaw had once again changed. New allotments had sprung up in corners of the flattened ghetto grounds, on boulevards and in courtyards in the constant attempt to augment an ever-diminishing food supply. The streets were crowded with ragged, begging children, with impromptu markets, and with the noise of trolleys and carts and improvised rickshaws. Cars announced Germans. Their round-ups had become more assiduous and frequent than ever as they hunted the few Jews who had escaped the last days of the ghetto and the Polish Resistance who, under orders from London Headquarters, helped them. Inspired by the Jewish Uprising, the activity of the partisans increased in the coming months. Prisoners were rescued from German convoys, ammunition dumps were raided, high-ranking German officers assassinated, shipments of Nazi gold and currency captured. These acts brought in their train ever fiercer reprisals.

My mother, grandmother and brother are riding in the front part of a trolley. They are smartly turned out. They need to be to travel in the German section of the tram. Hania's demeanour is rather severe. Her curly hair is forced back from her pretty face in stiff waves. She wears a tailored suit. She looks a little imperious, certainly sophisticated. As the trolley rattles through the busy streets, she spies a rickshaw coming up beside them. Sitting behind the cycling driver is her brother. She waves gaily. She points Adek out to the others and for a moment they all wave. They are delighted to see him, but they do not leap off the trolley to embrace him. They do not realise that they will never see him again. Instead they think how good it is that they have managed successfully to lose track of each other in this last year. They also think that now that the Americans are at last in Europe, it cannot be much longer before they are all together again.

Before that can happen though, they must change addresses once more. This time it was Sara's doing. In their new apartment, she had been looking after Staszek while Hania worked. But she had been looking after him too effusively. One of the neighbours had seen her chasing after her charge with a spoon, following him into the courtyard and begging him to eat. This seems to be a universal signal of Jewish maternal behaviour and the neighbour had come to Hania to say that her maid was certainly Jewish. The neighbour was terrified. She claimed she couldn't sleep at night for fear of what would happen to them all if they were found with a Jew in their midst.

Hania determined they must all quickly move further afield and into separate accommodation once more. She left her job without giving notice. Having seen an advertisement for lodgings in the outlying suburb of Sadyba, she went there. The

streets were quiet, almost rural after the tumult of the city
centre. There was a child playing outside number 44 Ulica
Zielona and she asked him for Pan Stanislaw Latko. The boy
told her his father would be home from work in a few hours'
time. He worked in a large Polish-German enterprise as an
accountant. Hania walked and waited, assessed the streets, the
woman next door pinning up her washing. When Pan Latko
returned, he showed her the two rooms of his flat he was let-
ting out. They overlooked a deep back garden. Staszek could
play there, out of harm's way, Hania thought. Pan Latko's son,
Andrzej, only some four years older, would be a friend. Both
father and son seemed pleasant.

'My son and I will move in tomorrow,' Hania said with her
lightning decisiveness.

'I'll need references.'

'References!'

When my mother recounts this episode, her face and body
take on a pose of wounded virtue. Her back stiffens, a single
eyebrow arches, her eyes speak insult, her lips quiver slightly
then round in astonishment. 'You'll need references, Pan
Latko? Here I am, a lady on her own, moving in with you, a
man. Don't you think I should be the one to ask for references?'

'So there is no husband?' Pan Latko gives her a small knowing smile.

'My husband runs a cosmetics factory in Warsaw. He's very
busy. He'll join us on weekends when he can. Meanwhile my
son needs a quiet environment.'

The very next day Hania and Staszek moved in. They were
now once again Kowalski. Within a short time Sara, too, had

a new housekeeping job in a second German household. Her fastidiousness as well as her culinary skills were a distinct boon. Meanwhile, Aron found accommodation near the small Sadyba lake, but he didn't visit the Latko house.

During one of the evening meals which they increasingly shared, Pan Latko asked Hania why. In the candlelight – this was not one of the three evenings on which electricity was permitted – she laughed away the question with coquettish frivolity. She told him she was waiting for his hair to turn a little greyer. She had explained to her husband that she was lodging with an old man and Pan Latko hadn't yet quite made the grade.

In fact she was biding her time, waiting to ascertain how far she could trust her new environment. Soon she found out.

The Sadyba streets have the quality of a village and gossip is rife. Everyone is curious about Pan Latko's new tenant who gives them friendly smiles but is fundamentally reserved. In an attempt to break the crust of her diffidence, one of the neighbours tells Hania all about Pan Latko, a nice enough widower, indeed an object of desire. But – she lowers her voice to a stage whisper – it is rumoured that his wife was Jewish. 'Jewish! Can you believe it!'

Hania receives this information without batting a long eyelash.

'And he must have a penchant for Jewish women,' the neighbour adds. 'That's why he's never taken up with anyone else.'

Hania lets it pass, but she realises that the tongues have probably already started wagging about her potential

Jewishness – given that Pan Latko seems to be so fond of her. She weighs up the risks and that weekend arranges for Kazik, her husband, to visit. Few, apart from Pan Latko, whom she now senses is utterly reliable, will see him for very long, but everyone will know that a husband really does exist.

By the end of that summer, Kazik is visiting most weekends. He takes the boys swimming. Occasionally, Sara comes round – she always chooses the Sabbath – and cooks them an evening meal. Given that she insists, availability willing, on making stuffed carp – *gefilte fish* – Hania suspects that Pan Latko must realise they are Jewish. Yet he never utters a word about it. Life takes on a semblance of normality. Hania shops and barters for food, cooks and watches Staszek and Andrzej play raucous games of cowboys and Indians in the back garden with the other children. She is frugal in her habits – any scrap of paper or food is conserved for future use – a habit which returns to her in old age.

Kazik has an occasional drink and chat with Latko and the neighbours. He helps to dig an irrigation ditch for one of them. They all seem to get on well. But it is a parody of the norm: every Sunday, Hania takes Staszek by the hand and despite his tugs in the opposite direction, drags him to church.

Come winter and drama strikes. Hania has sewn all their moveable worldly wealth – savings and jewellery – into the lining of her capacious muff. This is safer than leaving things at home. Raids have become more frequent again. Now the Germans are looking for partisans, underground leaflets, home army news-sheets. One day, the muff is left on the trolley bus. Hania is distraught. When she tells Aron, he says there is nothing to be done. It is too dangerous to go in search of it. They'll certainly rouse suspicion, be arrested. Hania refuses loss. She rides to the trolley depot. She talks to drivers and supervisors. The muff is miraculously returned to her, all its treasure intact.

Hania is to refuse loss throughout her life. She is lucky, a special being. Nothing is ever lost that cannot be found again – keys, a lone sock, my daughter's school blazer, her brother. She puts the same energy into retrieving lost objects as she puts into shoring up omnipotence. If something is truly lost, then it can only be because it has been stolen. Responsibility for the bad, the evil, must always lie on the outside, not in any passive neglect. The war ratified her. It is probably what made her into such a durable survivor.

One weekend early in 1944, my father fails to check in. For two days and then a third, he vanishes from view. Even curfews don't bring him back. Hania goes surreptitiously to his lodgings. Not a sign. For the first time since her father's death, she experiences serious panic. She has nowhere to turn. She can only wait. And wait.

Aron, alias Kazik Zabłocki, alias Kazimierz Kowalski, has been arrested on the street. He doesn't know if someone has informed on him. It doesn't matter now. He is taken to the fateful Aleje Szucha, the Gestapo Headquarters, from which it is known few ever return alive.

He is locked in an underground cell, then interrogated, then beaten, then interrogated and beaten. He is bullishly passive. He plays the simple, honest man who has little to say and less to admit. He keeps pointing to his papers, his *Kennkarte*, and his baptismal certificate. He is respectful. He uses his modicum of German. When his trousers are pulled down and the material evidence is clear for all to witness, he has his story ready. Before the war, he was subject to a recurrent ailment. The only remedy was an operation. Hence his missing foreskin. The operation was performed in a large Warsaw hospital. He names a doctor, long-vanished. Unfortunately, the hospital's documentation can certainly not be retrieved. It was bombed in the early days of the war. He repeats this story over and over again until it takes on an aura of truth from the sheer blandness of the repetition. Two of the Gestapo officers believe him. Two do not. An SS doctor is called in.

The doctor takes Aron into a separate room. He examines him cursorily. 'Right,' he says. 'An operation.' He lowers his voice. 'If I were you, I'd hotfoot it to Germany. You'll be safer there. None of you left.'

Aron cannot believe his ears. He listens as the doctor states his verdict to the officers. And then he is booted from the interrogation room. Something, some grim humour, some tempting of fate, makes him go back, despite the foul temper of his escort. He knocks at the door and when it opens, he asks for his hat. 'Your hat!' the officer rails at him. 'You're in Gestapo Headquarters and you're in this situation and you ask for your hat!'

'It's cold out,' Aron murmurs, ever the honest fool. The hat is flung at him and he is escorted to the gate.

Maybe it was the hat which saved him – prevented him from being followed.

Throughout his life, my father was convinced that the Gestapo doctor who secured his freedom was, in fact, a disguised Jew. He couldn't bring himself to believe that a German had recognised him – and he was certain that he had been recognised – and set him free. His internal logic was the opposite of my mother's. He was never able to see himself as a special case, even as especially lucky. He never told this story as if he had acted with particular bravery. He told it as a story of solidarity. If he had been spared, it was because a brother had spared him, a fellow Jew who had achieved the cleverest of masquerades. And, like a cat who feels his nine lives are running out, the incident with the Gestapo only served to increase Aron's fear.

Through the spring and early summer months of that year, my parents' existence took on a tense ordinariness. Then, at 5 p.m. on August 1, 1944, the Warsaw Uprising erupted. As the Soviet army beat back the Germans and neared the city, all factions of the Polish Resistance joined forces to oust the Nazis. For my mother, it was the most terrifying part of the war. For my father there was a sense of partial release: at last, something was changing. Or so it seemed at first.

Only 2,500 members of the largely civilian Polish army were properly equipped. Against them stood a Nazi force 15,000 strong, backed by air power. In the first few days of the uprising, the partisans managed to capture gas, electric and water works. Using the sewers for troop movements, they fought with mad bravery in streets and courtyards and on bridges. And they died. Died behind makeshift barricades. Died running through sewers poisoned by Nazi gas bombs and in the debris of bombed and burned streets. By August 6, all Warsaw was in flames. After sixty-three days of fighting, and none of the hoped-for help from the Russians who had deliberately halted their advance in the suburb of Praga, 200,000 citizens lay dead. The rest of the starving, battered population was expelled from a city transformed into a rubble heap.

My parents and brother huddled in shelters or cellars as the sirens blared and the bombs fell. Trapped elsewhere in Warsaw, Sara was unreachable. There was no food except for what the small garden could provide. Leaving home was a danger, but so was staying in. Apart from the bombing, there were the constant raids. My brother and Andrzej both remember the Nazis knocking at the door of their suburban house and bursting in to hunt partisans. The entire male population between the ages of sixteen and fifty was suspect. In front of the house next door, Staszek saw a man shot, the blood pouring out of him far redder than he had imagined, far redder than the red on the armband which announced a member of the resistance army. Their neighbour, the one who carried tales about Jewish wives, stood on her balcony and shouted prayers to the Virgin Mary above the din of the planes. Pan Latko railed at her: 'she prays to be saved from the Nazis, but she's quite willing to send them Jews to be shot.'

One day, when the alarm went, my mother insisted that they all hide in the cellar rather than in the garden bunker. Insisted with such ferocity that the men and children obeyed. I can see her, can feel the unanswerable power of her determination: her blue eyes are lifted to the skies or somewhere above

her fellows to the spot where she locates her instinctual authority. Her lips move in a torrent of suasive language, as she takes
Staszek and little Andrzej by the hand and urges them down
the stairs into darkness. Short of brute force, nothing can stop
her. With grudging shrugs, the men follow.

Hania's doggedness kept them in the cellar so long that Aron
and Pan Latko had to steal upstairs to warm thin soup for the
complaining children. When they all finally emerged from its
dank confines, they found that the outdoor bunker had suffered a direct hit. Everyone in it was dead. The house next door
was in flames, the spiteful neighbour gone. 'From now on, you
take over as Commander,' Pan Latko said to my mother.
'You've saved our lives. Now we all follow your instincts and
listen to no one else.'

It is from this episode that I date my mother's continuing
certainty that her instincts are always right and must needs be
followed. In my childhood there was never any possibility of
arguing with her absolute conviction. When we, or particularly
my father, tried to, this story was resurrected as proof of her
infallible instinct. And on the whole, we followed her will –
like that small band on Ulica Zielona.

In the first week of October, just days after the crushed
Polish army settled for POW status, they were all alive to be
ripped from their beds in the middle of the night. As the
men were separated from the women, my mother heard
Latko calling after her, 'Pani Hanka, Pani Hanka,' as if she
were a talisman not to be given up. They were marched by
the Nazis to their first evacuation site – the Sadyba fortress.

Remaining able-bodied Warsawians were now to be shipped to labour camps in Germany. Fifteen thousand people crowded into the Sadyba fort where they huddled for two days before being marched to a station and shuttled to Pruszków. Here they were herded behind barbed wire in the railway yard my father had hoped never to see again. He was certain that this time it would finally prove his grave.

Hania was aghast at the conditions in the detention camp – the stench, the lack of toilets, the heave and cry of humanity crowded behind barbed wire. She was also desperate. Only one thing was clear to her. She had to get them all out of here. The need made her heroic. Tugging Staszek by the hand, she approached a German officer. She had to find her husband, she told him. Absolutely had to. He had all their remaining money – which was in fact hidden on her person – and she had been left alone with a sick child. Please. He had to help her.

Perhaps he had a child at home, perhaps he knew the war was drawing to an end and he would have to account for his sins, my mother later said: in any event, he helped. He walked through the men's detention site and shouted, 'Kowalski, Kowalski.'

Hearing his name called by a German officer, Aron prepared to meet his death. Instead, he found himself in front of a weeping Hania and Staszek. 'How can I possibly survive on my own?' Hania pleaded with the officer. 'Do what you like,' the German answered. 'I'm not looking.' To mark his words, he turned away.

Hania quickly wrapped her scarf around the entirety of Aron's head, leaving only his eyes exposed, as if he had suffered a head wound. They both feared recognition in Pruszków: Jews could still be shot outright. Then, too, a wounded man would not be hustled on to a train bound for a German work camp. As they approached the tracks, Hania asked another German about trains. He said there was one about to come in. He would make sure they got on it. They had no idea about destination. The important thing was to get away.

The freight car was so closely packed, movement was impossible. In the growing heat, Aron forgot himself and moved his makeshift bandage of a scarf to one side. 'Look at that,' a woman shouted. 'He's not even wounded. Why is he here? My husband was packed off to Germany.'

The family edged away as best they could to a far corner of the carriage. Eventually the train creaked to a halt. They leapt off into sunlight so bright, it dazzled the eyes. The sign on the small station read Sadow. On the platform, they spied a priest. My mother rushed up to him, told him they were evacuees from Warsaw, explained their plight. Her husband was wounded, her child unwell. There had been no food for days. She had a little money ... Please, could he help them in any way?

There and then the priest wrote a letter of introduction for them to a peasant family in a neighbouring village and directed them to the right road. They walked. The priest's letter in hand, they received a warm welcome.

The house with its two whitewashed rooms felt like heaven. The peasant family had three small children. They lived in one room, Hania, Kazik and Staszek in the other. They slept on straw and horsehair mattresses around the fireplace. Whatever food there was – bread, potatoes, cucumber, milk, cabbage, the occasional egg – was shared out between them. Everyone worked hard. My father's fear began to subside a little. No more days filled only with the endless stretch of streets and their treacherous inhabitants. He enjoyed this simple hard-working life of the village.

Staszek did too, for somewhat different reasons. Suddenly my brother's memory enters the narrative as a more consistent voice. He is over five – a precocious hothouse child, alert, slightly wild, quick to see plots and imagine machinations as complicated and intense as the ones he has already lived through. At my prodding Staszek, now Stanley, recounted his early life to me over a week of memory work, partly spent in the solitude of a Cambridge flat. It was the first time I had attempted to elicit memories from him and I was struck both by his ability to recall vivid detail and by the fact that his remembering didn't always coincide with my parents'. Though they dip into the same pool of images, his memories bear his own particular stamp. They are boldly sexual and have a boy's own story frenzy. But then, those war days were ones in which boys lived such stories.

Staszek made friends with two other boys in the village. They were the sons of Engineer Pietrowski, a professional who had moved to the countryside for security. The boys had beautiful toy soldiers which Staszek coveted – soldiers in bright red and blue uniforms. One day he pinched the soldiers. His mother found them and insisted that he return them. Staszek was angry and humiliated. He stole back to the Pietrowski house after dark and chucked the soldiers one by one through the post-slot. In the morning, they were inadvertently stepped on and broken. No one would ever play with them again. Or perhaps they were merely forgotten. In the village now that winter had set in, there were real soldiers. Big Russian soldiers with big machine guns. Battles raged in the woods behind the village between the Russians and the Germans.

The Russians told the villagers it would be wise to move further back from the Front. They walked through the icy night towards a neighbouring hamlet. In the fields, they found a wounded Wehrmacht officer. He begged for water. 'Kill him,' said Staszek. 'No, no,' Hania insisted. The man had to be helped. He was human too. She gave him water. They half-carried, half-dragged the German back towards the road where they happened upon a Wehrmacht vehicle. Here they left him and carried on towards the next village.

They slept on straw on the floor of a mill. It was very cold. They stayed there for several days, until word came that the Germans were retreating.

In the woods some three kilometres behind Sadow, there had been a big battle, particularly brutal, my brother remembers, because part of General Vlasov's Ukrainian collaborationist army fought there and, given that they were Soviet turncoats, the Russians treated them with especial venom. The men of the village went out into the woods to scavenge. They found bodies piled in snow and unexploded shells. From an abandoned German vehicle, Aron brought back a rucksack filled with schnapps and black bread. Staszek and the boys also secretly went out to scavenge. They dared each other on, further and further into the woods. Staszek found hand grenades, a Schmeisser half-hidden in snow. He stored these in the cellar of the house until one of the boys squealed on him and his growing arms collection was confiscated by his father.

A Russian soldier came to camp in their house. He smoked pungent Zahorka tobacco rolled in newspaper. A member of the frontline liberation troops, he was kind and well-behaved, not like the later reserve troops who were prone to rape and pillage. His hosts even convinced him to trade his horse for vodka. They desperately needed a horse for their fields. The man agreed.

My mother too used to tell a story about this particular Russian soldier. In her usual friendly way, she chatted to him as she went about her tasks. She was curious about Russians, never having met any at close quarters before. This one was a Georgian, dark-haired and ruddy with mellow eyes. He looked Jewish, she thought. As a way of testing the waters, one day after he had been with them for some weeks, Hania asked him whether there were any Jews in Georgia. She wanted a sense of this new power they now had to contend with. She also wondered whether he was, in fact, a Jew.

The Georgian grinned at her and with a little sneer told her if she wanted to find any Jews, she'd have to look a lot higher up in the military hierarchy. No ordinary soldiers like him were ever Jews, oh no. Taken aback, Hania decided that the Russians were no better than anyone else. Nothing had changed. They had to be as careful as ever. In some ways she felt the Russians were even worse than the Germans: they had no manners.

*

Towards the middle of January 1945, just after the liberation of
Warsaw by the Russians on the 17th, Aron set off for Pruszków
to reconnoitre. He wore a sheepskin-lined coat and wooden
clogs. The temperature was well below zero and the snow was
thick on the ground. He took black bread and a bottle of vodka
with him. He walked along the train tracks which led towards
Warsaw. He walked and walked, sleeping when and where he
could. He had about two hundred kilometres to cover.
Sometimes he managed a lift in a horse-drawn cart for a stretch
of road.

When he reached his home town, everything was both the
same and radically different. Where the Germans had been,
there were now Russians patrolling the streets in their jeeps.
The desolate evacuees had disappeared from the railway
yards. But the shops were closed. There was nothing to sell
and little to buy it with. The faces he crossed in the street
were grim – pinched with poverty and fatigue and defeat. The
Russians might be saviours. They were also new oppressors.
Aron began his search for family members and friends. It was
principally that he had come for. He found no one. No Jews.
Not yet, he told himself. He was the first back. The war was
still not over.

At last he located a Polish friend, the owner of a brickworks,
and a single Jewish woman, who was still in hiding and initially
refused to know him. Despite the rout of the Germans from
the area, everyone was cautious. The Polish friend told him that
he had heard that old man Kramarski, Aron's mother's rich
cousin in Tarczyn, was still alive. Not only alive, but doing very
well. His pretty daughter Cesia had taken up with a Russian

colonel and the colonel fixed matters for him: ousted the
Volksdeutsche who had taken over the large grain mill in which
Kramarski was a partner with a Borensztejn cousin at the start
of the war. Now the mill was back with Kramarski.

Aron makes his way to Tarczyn. It is a dawdle, only some
twenty-five kilometres. When he arrives at the Kramarski
house, no one at first recognises him. He is a shade of his
former self. And he looks like what he has become, a destitute,
balding, and hardly clean peasant. When the family realise who
he is, there is rejoicing. The stories come out with the vodka.
Kramarski and his daughter have survived the last years in a
bunker in the fields behind the town. He paid the peasants to
keep them and bring them food. The local lady of the manor
was a partisan and sympathetic to Jews. And now, he does
indeed have his mill back. And it is full of flour confiscated
from the usurping *Volksdeutsche*. He slaps Aron heartily on the
back. Aron is to come and work for him. He needs reliable
agents to find clients and to set the business back on its feet.
His guts tell him it will be a good, if tricky time, for business.
He lowers his voice. The Russians are okay, but they're not
businessmen and one has to watch them.

Two days later, cart and horse at the ready, Aron starts trading. Currencies are unstable and unreliable. There are marks
and rubles and zloty and the occasional dollar. Only the last has
any value. And poverty is everywhere. But deals can be done.
After all, he is trading in the very stuff of life. By March, he has
a room and clients throughout the vicinity. He also has suffi-
cient funds to send for Hania and Staszek. He arranges for a

Jewish woman, who like them has survived as a Pole and is a tough manoeuvrer, to fetch them from Sadow.

Staszek finds the journey excruciating in its slowness. They travel mostly by night. They travel in freight cars that hardly seem to move. They travel in trucks and in carts. At last they arrive in Pruszków. Their new home is a single room shared with two distant young cousins of Aron's, Helenka and Marisa, who have also lived through the war disguised as Poles. Hania doesn't seem too fond of Marisa. Staszek hears his parents arguing about her. Later, when he knows what these things mean, he assumes that his father has been sleeping with the woman.

My brother's childhood memories have a grammar of sexuality about them: few relations can be parsed without it. That doesn't mean that on occasion he might not be right.

The single room soon grows into two. The apartment takes on the aspect of a refugee centre. Aron's travels in grain also act as a communications network. Whatever returnees there are to and through Pruszków stop at the flat. They all have stories of tremendous hardship. Most have come from labour camps in Russia or Soviet Asia, where they were transported, having fled east across the River Bug into Soviet-occupied Poland at the start of the war. Others have survived immured behind secret walls or in bunkers or ditches. Or lived in disguise, like them. Staszek listens. The stories are recounted with matter-of-fact swiftness. They are more often than not simply a way of catching up, of situating the other and embracing in a fraternity of endurance. Along with the stories, there is a search for kin. Where was Abraham last seen? What happened to Marek?

For the Passover celebrations in April, the first open ones

since the war began, the small flat is full. Amongst the guests are two Russian soldiers – Jews, who want to desert and go to Palestine. Aron finds them clothes, gives them money and a lift west out of town. Some years after the war, my parents receive a letter of thanks from them. They have reached Israel, having first made their way to Germany and spent some time in a refugee centre there.

On May 2, Berlin falls to Soviet and Polish troops. On the 8th, war in Europe is formally over. Amongst the few remaining Pruszków Jews, jubilation is muted. Official confirmation of the existence of the Nazi killing camps makes rejoicing impossible. Millions are dead.

For Aron and Hania, the war ended earlier and hasn't ended at all. Nothing has returned to normal. Sara has miraculously come back from the ruins of Warsaw, but the rest of their nearest kin are still missing, including the relative whose hoard of textiles kept them from penury. Aron has tried to find him in order to settle this extraordinary debt. To no avail. They have begun to believe the worst, begun to believe that everyone is dead. Though Hania is adamant that her brother will still turn up.

Part of the sense of the war not being over is due to the presence of the Russians. They are meant to be a liberating army, but they seem to be here to stay. Their secret policemen, dressed as army officers, are all-powerful. The best one can say for them is that – officially, at least – they do not seem to be against the Jews. The family is friendly with them. The Russians need flour and Aron needs whatever business as well as protection he can get. As the reach of his trading expands, he often arranges for a bemedalled Soviet officer to man the front of his truck or train carriage to see his shipment safely through. It is through the help of a Soviet officer, too, that the family retrieve their old apartment from the reluctant Polish policeman who has taken it over.

Aron's travels gradually make him aware that fighting is still going on here and there in woods and villages. The Poles are in a bitter mood. Splintered in their allegiances to Communist and nationalist factions, they now fight each other as well as the Soviets. Nor do many of them feel kindly towards the 300,000 or so Jews who slowly filter home from Russia, other parts of Poland and the various countries to which war has banished them. The Poles don't want to give back the houses or businesses they have acquired. Nor do many of the Poles returning from labour camps in Germany have anywhere to go. Everyone is devastated by the destruction the country has suffered. Apart from Krakow, most of the towns and cities are in ruins.

Warsaw is worst afflicted. Aron goes there to explore and to find traces of missing relatives. He registers with the Jewish Committee. Like everyone else, he posts messages on the ghostly paper-littered facades of buildings. His messages list the names of the disappeared and indicate where Aron can be found. He walks the scorched shells of streets where men and women sift rubble with bare hands in an effort to construct temporary shelters. The city is unrecognisable. Beneath the charred mass of buildings, he thinks he can sniff the stench of rotting bodies.

*

By the summer, Aron's business is prospering. He returns home
from his expeditions, his cases laden with money. The old
apartment is always crowded with friends and acquaintances.
Aron and Hania are generous with their relative wealth and
help those who have helped them. Much to Staszek's consternation, they are even kind to the Jewish ghetto policeman,
whom he has heard Aron say time and again he would never
forgive. He can't fathom what to the adults is a necessary Jewish
solidarity – after so much death. He can't really understand his
new designation as Jew.

Pan Latko and his son, Andrzej, come and amidst much
embracing, there is a moment's consternation when Hania
reveals they are Jewish. 'Really,' she insists and laughs at his
scepticism. Later, as a signal of her triumph as actress and
Aryan, Hania will repeatedly mimic Pan Latko's grumble of
continued disbelief – 'What is this? Suddenly everybody wants
to be Jewish!'

Pan Oselinski visits too. He is treated as an honoured guest.
The best food is provided. The vodka flows. But one day
Oselinski surprises them by saying that he will no longer be
coming to see them.

'Why?' Hania asks.

Embarrassment tinged with anger is evident in his features.
'In the present climate,' he explains, 'if anyone found out that
I'd helped Jews during the war, I'd be massacred immediately.'

Things are better, my mother thinks; but things are far from
good.

In the middle of all this, Hania has a new and ardent
admirer, a KGB (or then NKVD) colonel my brother vividly

remembers as Sacha. When the officer can't be at his lady-love's side, he takes little Staszek for rides in his jeep. Staszek is his pet and he is encouraged to point his finger at any German collaborators he spies en route. Staszek is more than willing to comply. He savours the notion of revenge and he has heard the grown-ups talking over past crimes.

'There, that one!' he points with joy.

'Right, that one,' his handsome companion echoes.

Even today, my brother is certain that some of his designated collaborators disappeared.

Staszek liked this Russian with his smart uniform and smarter car. For Hania, things were somewhat trickier and potentially dangerous. The officer paid no heed whatsoever to the existence of Aron. Sacha wanted to marry her, to take her and Staszek back to the Soviet Union with him. He had even written to his mother to that effect and shown Hania the letter.

When my mother saw this letter, she later told me, she was seriously worried. She had had no intention of igniting a grand passion, she claimed. She had simply been friendly. And now she had no idea how to handle matters. If she was openly hostile to this powerful officer, things could go badly for all of them. Russian tempers were known to be erratic and all of them counted on the man for his protection. But if she continued to be amicable, he would persist in his attentions. Her dreams hardly included running off to the Soviet Union.

My father – who always sat a little more stiffly than usual during the recounting of this particular episode of their lives – solved the dilemma. He decided to move the family to Łódź. Apart from its razed ghetto, the city was mostly intact. By

September, they were established in a fine apartment on Ulica Legionow. Hania was five months pregnant. She was pregnant with me.

For years, in his Oedipal resentment of his intrusive little sister, my brother would contend during rows that I was the product of my mother's affair with the KGB colonel. A curly-haired Russian with a star on his cap and dark almond-shaped eyes was my real father. My mother, of course, could only deny this. In my moments of rebellion, I rather relished the idea – though I would have liked a different mother too. We'll never know the truth. What we do know is that family romance is a rich terrain for fantasy. Perhaps Staszek, always and ever a jealous guardian of maternal affections, would have preferred a military jeep to a flour-laden truck. Or perhaps he would simply and rightly have been happier if a family closeness honed in terror had not been ruptured by an interloper who could only displace him.

On Site

Early on a cold and drizzly morning Monica and I set out for Warsaw's mainline station and take the train to Łódź, Poland's second largest city, which lies 130 kilometres south-west of the capital. The train carriages, with their separate compartments, are crowded. No one surprises us with a public smile. Maybe there isn't much to smile about on this grey day. The conductors, who regularly check our tickets, are diffident to the point of surliness. Łódź is an hour and fifty minutes of fields and forests away.

In the second half of the nineteenth century, Łódź became a major centre of the textile industry, exporting cotton, wool and linen throughout Eastern Europe. It was Manchester to Warsaw's London, a thriving industrial capital. Between the wars, its Jewish population numbered some 250,000 – over a quarter of its total. At the start of the Second World War, the city was incorporated into the Reich: Poles and Jews were 'resettled' with rapid brutality. Some 70,000 Jews alone were killed or hunted from the city, their wealth appropriated by the Reich. A ghetto was established in February 1940. Here, in an area of four square kilometres, 164,000 Jews were immured. By the end of the war, after the mass deportations to Chelmno and Auschwitz, only around 800 remained alive.

As we leave the train station, Monica and I feel as if nothing much has changed, except for the worse, in the physical character of Łódź since the early twentieth century. The looming apartment blocks are covered in a thick coat of industrial grime, although the town centre has begun to be affected by the post-Communist clean-up: a pedestrian zone sports a smattering of new cafés and repainted buildings. My guidebook doesn't seem to think the city of my birth even merits an entry.

No matter. We are here on business. Through Monica's cousin, Joasia, we have been put in touch with a lawyer who knows how to navigate his way through a bureaucracy of registry offices and city archives. For the first time in my life I may at last acquire a birth certificate, let alone other family documents.

We follow the directions we have been given, reach Plac Dombrowskiego and walk along a street of once imposing and now sadly run-down office buildings. Number 57 is no better than its neighbours, but once we have crossed the threshold, everything is different. We are in a set of austere and impeccably furnished offices. The dark furniture gleams with a loving coat of polish. A tall young man strides towards us. His bearing is military, his white-blond hair shortly cropped, his fair cheeks tinged with pink. He is scrubbed and smartly suited. He almost clicks his heels as he puts out a hand to each of us and enunciates his name. Stanislaw Piotr Kubiak, a trainee advocate, has been assigned to us by his chief. We are ushered into a second office, one which could have been dreamt by a Dutch master, except for the huge romantic landscape which hangs there, its heavy, ornamented frame challenging the wall for solidity. Kubiak is formal, courteous and precise. He recites our itinerary to us in near-perfect English, a language he has explained he cannot speak, though his German is much better. A quick phone call, an exchange of pleasantries, and he leads us out. So much does he bring to mind romantic tales of Polish cavalry officers, that for a moment, I have an image of horses awaiting us.

Instead, there is a taxi. We judder over cobbled streets criss-crossed by trolley rails and pull up in front of an open courtyard. Atop one of the dilapidated buildings at its far end, a giant sign advertises BOSCH. I am a little startled to find that we are heading for the doorway directly beneath it. Could the home of the Łódź Jewish community really be hidden behind a leading German trademark – the very one which in French stands in for all Germans? It is. Discreetly positioned beneath BOSCH, a small plaque announces the community centre, the Gmina. I can feel my father growing various shades of livid.

Inside, the stairwell walls are dark and lead-painted, with a thin leaf motif etched in black on their bottom half. Nothing, it would seem, has been touched since the building's original construction. There is a smell of damp which, as we open the door to the first-floor premises, merges with the pungency of stewing meat and thick gravy. Behind a hatch, a half-dozen old people sit and eat and chatter. These are a few of Łódź's remaining 700 or so Jews, most of them old now, survivors.

The hot meals are a charitable service funded by World Jewish Relief, as is the work of the community, which includes holding weekly and holiday services at the synagogue on Rewolucja 1905 Street, recently rebuilt with the support of the Ronald S. Lauder Foundation. This apart, the Gmina also runs the Bracka Street Cemetery, and maintains its archives. These are the reason we have come.

We go into a small office, crowded with people and desks and the mechanical stutter of a fax. Two old paintings adorn the distempered walls, one of a rabbi in full ritual garb, the second of a Chevra Kaddisha, that traditional charitable society which existed in all Jewish communities and was responsible in the first instance for the burial of the dead. There is a woman behind one of the desks. Vivid in hair and gesture, she deals first with a couple from Israel, then with an old Pole who is trying to settle some outstanding bill, all this amidst intermittent phone calls and more knocks at the door and a wave to a young man, who makes his way to a second desk, rifles through it and presents me with a piece of paper. I stare at it in consternation. It takes me a few moments to realise that this is my grandmother Sara's death certificate. *Karta Zgonu.* Our lawyer has been too polite to mention death.

The document gives me a great deal of unknown information – forgotten by my mother. I learn my grandmother's wartime name – Juliana Ambroziak; a date of birth which may or may not be accurate – May 15, 1882; a place of birth, Biala Podlaska; and a father's name, Szulim Baila. I also learn that she died of a brain haemorrhage in a Łódź hospital on October 13, 1948. A mourner's expression on his face, our advocate tells me that unfortunately the hospital where she died no longer exists. I shrug. I am thrilled by this document, despite the sadness it evokes. I have two copies made of it – one for myself, one for my mother.

We are still waiting to have a word with the vivacious woman behind the desk. Kubiak's impatience struggles with his good manners. It comes to me that he doesn't know how to behave amidst this foreign species that Jews in a group must be to him. Though he would possibly like to, he can't be officious. Then, too, Monica and I are unknown territory – his first clients from abroad, he has admitted to us.

When the woman is finally ready, she throws her arms up in the air and giggles. It is clear that despite the fact that Kubiak thinks he has arranged for everything, she has either forgotten or has no idea why we're still here. Kubiak explains that we're waiting for her to ring the person who will conduct us round the vast Jewish cemetery. With a wink, the woman picks up the phone, only to tell us a moment later, that he's gone to the dentist's. Tomorrow would be better. But we have no tomorrow in Łódź, so she picks up the phone again to arrange for the grave-keeper to show us round.

We are still sitting there. Kubiak nudges me and whispers that I should make a contribution for services rendered. I do so and in turn, the woman hands him a *yarmulke*, the head-covering he will need if he is to conduct himself according to Jewish practice in the cemetery. The colour on his cheekbones grows a little brighter, but he thanks her courteously. It is only as we leave that I realise the woman is the daughter of the man whose name I was given in London as a source of information about Jews in Łódź. I faxed but received no response. 'Oh faxes,' the woman laughs, waving an arm round the cluttered office. 'Too many of them.'

A taxi waits for us in the driveway. For once, we have hit upon a garrulous driver, who wants nothing more than to chat and to laugh and to show off his city. Like an East End cabby, he keeps up a steady repartee. Just outside the old Jewish quarter, he points to a mammoth building, an entire city block of encrusted chateau. This he tells us was the home of Poznanski, one of the richest of the city's nineteenth-century Jewish industrialists, whose name and philanthropic activities figure large in Łódź's history. With sparky gaiety, our cabby adds that apparently Poznanski wanted to cover the floor of one of his ballrooms in gold coin, but there wasn't enough in Łódź to supply him! Born of an admixture of truth and myth, money seems to attend most stories about Jews. Luckily, culture sometimes follows: the Poznanski Palace is now a museum.

We drive past a flat empty space, dotted here and there with desultory market stalls. This, our driver notes, was the old Jewish quarter and later the ghetto. Almost nothing is left of it. What houses were standing after the series of deportations were burnt for fuel. He used to play in the fields here as a child, he informs us. There too, where the oldest Jewish cemetery stood. That was ravaged by the Nazis and then destroyed after the war. Never mind, the Bracka Street Cemetery still stands – the largest Jewish cemetery in Europe. He adds this with a note of pride, as if dead Jews were somehow good Jews.

'Not as large as Auschwitz,' our young lawyer mutters in an acerbic reprimand.

There is silence after that. We turn left at a secondhand car dealer's and drive along a narrow pitted road. Countryside has overtaken us. To one side, there are fields and allotments; to the other, a long stretch of brick wall which abuts on an arched ornamental gate. We have arrived.

Near the gate is a pretty turn-of-the-century red-brick building, the keeper's house. We knock at the door. A dog howls and barks and leaps out at us, followed by a scruffy, dishevelled man with the surly countenance of a Shakespearean gravedigger. He isn't pleased to see us on his terrain, but he tramps through the gate of a second internal wall ahead of us, muttering '1948' beneath his breath like a mantra. He leads us past the monumental tombs and mausolea of Łódź's textile emperors – floral wrought-iron balustrades, polished black granite and white marble, a large Secessionist dome ornamented with vivid mosaic and bearing the name of Poznanski, who also, in 1892, donated the land on which the cemetery grew. Around these mausolea are the smaller headstones, some inscribed in Hebrew, some in Polish, many bearing the familiar motifs of open palms, or books, or candelabra, or birds, or ships with broken masts – all traditional symbols with precise meanings.

We look for a patch of 1948 tombs. The air is moist, the vegetation high and sparkling with cobwebs which cling to our clothes. Leaves rustle, enclose us in a whispering cupola. I have always liked cemeteries, I don't quite know why. I feel at peace in them as if it is good to rest in earth after the stormy upheavals of life. Maybe I came here as a toddler to pay my final respects to my grandmother. I would like to find her now and say to her, as a child might, 'Hello, Granny, we've come from far away just to say hello.' But it isn't so easy. The grave-keeper can't seem to find the tomb. He trudges here and there, pokes moss with a stick, always and ever muttering to himself.

Some of these trees might not have been here then. Many were pulled up for firewood during the war. The cemetery formed part of the ghetto. In a site named the Ghetto Fields are the mass graves of some fifty thousand people who died in the epidemics which raged through that tragic quarter during the war years. I trip over a piece of curved iron wedged in the ground and remember that the Germans forbade the Jews tombstones, so instead bedframes or low cement posts were used as grave-markers. My granny has a stone, I am certain of that. But on so many of them, the writing is obliterated, erased by time. The gravekeeper throws his hands up in the air. He has had enough. He can't find Sara Lipszyc.

I wander around for a while on my own and conjure up images of the past. I imagine my parents walking here, their growing sense of doom about Poland. Their desire to leave now that all the old are gone, to shed the past with its brutal streets and bloodied fields. My father is thirty-five, my mother thirty-two or thereabouts, neither as old as I am now. They want a new life. They want to lose the dead.

Maybe that's all I'm doing here in Poland, too. Losing the dead all over again.

Certainly, my grandmother's grave is nowhere in sight.

I catch up with the others at the gates. Our lawyer asks us what, as Jews, we feel being here.

As Jews?

I don't know how to answer him. I don't seem to have

feelings as a group. All the question does is trap me in the dynamic of 'otherness'. Perhaps he expects me to feel anger, moral outrage. Perhaps I should. But so much time has passed. All I feel is sorrow.

We are in a taxi again, hurtling through unpeopled streets towards the address of my birth. My sense of anticipation has returned. This time surely, the 'madeleine' effect will catch me by surprise and catapult me into childhood sights and scents. Maybe there will still be a bakery there. I can already sniff the odour of yeast rising amongst the streets of heavy stone, see the soft little curving rolls, like dolls' hats, encrusted with sugar, the laced breads topped with poppy seeds. Yes.

The taxi turns into a desolate space where two other cabs are stationed. Our lawyer clears his throat. 'We're here.'

'Here,' I respond gaily.

'Yes, I didn't like to tell you.'

'Tell me what?'

'Well, number 55. It's been pulled down. This is it. Where it was.'

We are in a deep rectangular space between two apartment blocks. On both of the neighbouring walls, the traces of a sloping roof are visible – a large-upside down V just one floor beneath the adjoining roofs. A large, garish billboard cuts through the V of one of the walls. On it, a giant of a monster lifts the roof of a concert hall with his ogre's clutch. The caption advertises a radio station broadcasting music and news.

I have a sudden sense that all along I've been in the wrong

LOSING THE DEAD

novel. No Proustian full circles here, only a Borgesian labyrinth with an accumulation of disappearing objects – one house now a library, another a car park.

We walk along the turn-of-the-century street, straight and wide, flanked on either side with shabby grey buildings which must once have been light or painted in pastel shades. The iron grille-work of balconies dots the facades. An old-fashioned trolley clatters down rails set in cobblestones. There are no bakeries. From a balcony opposite, an old man watches us. Yesterday, our lawyer tells us, he came here and spoke to the people across the road to ask them about the fate of number 55. They were friendly at first, but when he rang them to see whether I might come and talk to them, they refused, afraid that we had come to claim property rights.

The anecdote saddens me almost more than the random disappearance of the family home. So many layers of fear and resentment, etched by a history of displacement – homes one is ousted from by war or occupation or politics.

Before we leave Łódź, our straight-backed young lawyer, altogether the model new Pole, asks me what I think I owe him for his work. Moral panic overtakes me. How much are a lost past and dead bodies worth? I want him to name the price. He doesn't want to. Whatever it's worth to me, he says. Whatever I think is fair.

I try to separate out the currencies of emotion and coin, the two different kinds of debt. I give him what I think is fair in coin. But debts aren't that easy to shed. Death is an irreversible currency. And I still feel guilty. I guess I feel guilty because I got away and I'm so very happy that I did.

Wartime and After

It is October 1945. Hania paces the capacious apartment in Ulica Legionow and occasionally pauses to look out of the window. She folds her hands across her rounded stomach where the baby kicks. She is worried. Aron has been away for days, far longer than foreseen. And there has been no word from him, despite the new telephone which adorns the side table.

She turns at her mother's footsteps behind her. She still cannot get used to the lank white hair and old woman's face which Sara brought back with her after their time of separation in the last year of the war.

'Still nothing,' Sara says. It is not a query. 'Maybe they've got him.'

'Who's got him?'

Sara shrugs.

She doesn't need to speak. Hania knows that the 'they' is a generalised authority which fits Germans or Russians or Poles. Sara is thinking about her son, not Aron. She only thinks about her son of whom there is still no sign. They have even had a visit from Adek's sister-in-law and her husband and children, who owe their lives to Adek. They wept in displaced gratitude on Sara's shoulder. But of Adek and his own wife and children, there is no news.

Sara is in a state of mourning without being properly able to mourn. There is no dead body. She will not give up the possibility that her son is alive. Instead she walks round in a shroud of depression so thick that it prevents her from seeing the new life forming inside Hania.

Hania affects a lightness more and more difficult to sustain. When the doorbell rings, she runs to answer it in wild relief.

The awaited message from Aron has come. She reads through it. Then, with only a cursory command to her mother to tend to Staszek when he returns from school, she takes her coat and leaves the house.

The following events are recounted solely by my brother. He is certain of their basis in fact and claims my ignorance of them is to do not only with my late arrival into family consciousness, but with my parents' wilful forgetting of shameful family dramas.

Aron is in Radom, a large town some fifty kilometres away. He is in jail. He has been arrested by the Russian military authority. The arrest is due neither to black-market dealings nor to any form of criminal activity. He has been arrested because he has been spending time with the General's mistress. The General wants no rivals. He is a jealous tyrant and he has had Aron locked up, as a preliminary to a more fatal punishment.

Somehow, in the fierceness of her pregnancy, Hania manages to locate the officer in question. She is Pana Kowalska again. For safety's sake in his business dealings Aron continues to use his acquired Polish name. Anti-Semitism is still rife. The time for honesty and straightforward transactions has not yet arrived. In my parents' case, it never really altogether does.

Hania throws herself at the officer's feet. She pleads for mercy. 'Pan Kowalski is a married man, about to be a father once again. You must be mistaken in your suspicions,' she tells the officer. 'He couldn't do this to me. Wouldn't. Not when I'm in this state. In any event, I couldn't survive as a widow. Please. We have enough widows.'

Hania triumphs once again. Out of pity or honour, the officer releases Kazik Kowalski. But he is barred from the precincts of Radom thereafter.

I narrate this incident because in family mythology it forms an apt parallel to Hania's alleged affair with the KGB colonel in Pruszków. It also gives something of the flavour of those early post-war years, their dangerous and anarchic play of military authority. It was a time of uncertain government, of viciously competitive politics and of harsh financial instability. The leader of Poland's Communist Party, Wladyslaw Gomulka, may have wanted to steer a Polish course to socialism, free of the stranglehold of Moscow, but he had been brought to power by Soviet might, and it was only with Soviet help that he could triumph over the revived Peasant Party and its allies on the nationalist right. In fact, many Poles wanted the equalising changes that Communism could bring: a land reform which broke up the huge estates and distributed them to the peasants; abolition of the upper house; nationalisation of core industries. But they didn't necessarily want them under the yoke of their ancient enemy.

Before the so-called 'free elections' that Yalta called for came in January 1947, Poland plunged into what was almost a civil war. Old factional enmities slipped into new ones, as the left, aided by the Soviet military and secret police, fought the nationalist right, abetted by the exile government in London. Towns and villages were raided, Soviet convoys ambushed, riots fomented, meetings broken up by mobs. Tens of thousands lost their lives. In Kielce, in July 1946, forty-two Jewish refugees from the Soviet Union on their way to Palestine, were brutally slaughtered by right-wing nationalists in what became known as the Kielce Pogrom, the most notorious in a series of similar anti-Semitic outbursts. It was as if the Nazis had normalised brutality, sanctioned Poles to behave towards Jews as inhuman creatures, beasts to be slaughtered.

This hideous incident, coming hard on the heels of fuller news of the killing camps, resulted in a wave of Jewish emigration. Of Kielce, the guilty right said it had been provoked by the left, whose leaders, after all, were Jews who had spent the war years in the hated Soviet Union. The insidious refrain linking Communists and Jews, hardly new, continued to play its part in Polish propaganda for many years. When the Stalin-guaranteed free elections of 1947 finally came, it was only with Soviet-style intercession. Thousands of nationalist activists, including 142 electoral candidates, were locked behind bars. A fifth of electoral districts – those where the nationalists were set to win – were disqualified. As a result, the Communist Bloc won 394 seats in Parliament against the nationalists' 28. Poland's post-war future was set.

After his taste of arbitrary Soviet power, not to mention the newest wave of anti-Semitism, my father was more than ever determined to leave Poland. Whenever he could over the coming years, he converted the zlotys he earned into dollars. He did this in several ways. One was to give Polish Jews in need zlotys, while their families in the United States paid some equivalent into his New York brother's bank account. Another was to make whatever transactions he could in 'hard' currencies – dollars or pounds. These he 'banked' in various secret sites in the apartment. The dollars in New York were intended to pay for passports. But American passports proved extremely difficult to come by.

Meanwhile, sometime in the early morning of January 4, 1946, I was born. My mother has always said that when she felt the first contractions coming on, she couldn't rouse my father, so deeply was he asleep. He'd had too much to drink the night before. Eventually, she succeeded, and he had to stagger out into the snow-laden night to find a car or cart and only then could they make the trek to the clinic where I was promptly born to his renewed snores. At first my mother wouldn't believe the midwife when she told her I was a girl. She had set her heart on a girl and it would be too great a good fortune for me to be one. Even my once again wakened father found it difficult to convince her of the fact. Showed the proof, guaranteed that this female child was indeed hers and didn't belong to someone else in the clinic, she was jubilant. They were both very happy. I was the signal of new life after too many deaths. A sign of hope and future promise. Maybe, too, I was the pledge of a marriage which had survived the terrors of war and the frenzy of its aftermath. For all their future rows and occasional vagaries, my parents stayed staunchly together.

I was taken home to an irascible brother and a depressed grandmother. My mother claims that she was frightened to leave me alone in a room with Staszek after she had once caught him with a pillow pressed over my face. These little hurdles of sibling life apart, I grew quickly into a post-war plumpness to match my mother's. Where there had been scarcity, there was now food and a great deal of it seemed to find its way into my mouth. Soon there were three women feeding me: a girl from the village of Sadow – with which cordial relations had been maintained – came to supplement mother and grandmother. Her name was Zosia and she became a great favourite of Staszek's.

He was seven and at school now, a local Communist school which he enjoyed. He seems particularly to have enjoyed taking part in the school contingent in demonstrations. These were mounted to counter the right-wing demos which always included a blare of anti-Semitic slogans. His full realisation that he was Jewish had only come recently. It must have produced not a little confusion, along with the new name, Borensztejn, which was now said to be the real name, though the others were still in use. All that, plus a mewling little sister, the cuckoo in the nest, must have been a great deal to bear. In the pictures of the time, he looks like a stern little boy, his bearing fiercely military, perhaps in imitation of all the soldiers who had paraded through his young life. In imitation, too, of the lost Adek whose heroism grew greater with each passing month and who haunted family life with an intractable power. If their saviour was dead, then they were all implicated in his death. Keeping hope alive against reason, was far better than the manacles of guilt. Adek would return.

Late in 1946 or at the beginning of 1947, Aron gave up the grain business to go into a manufacturing partnership, 'Łodska Konfekcja'. Suits were produced at the rate of 1,000 a week. In 1948, when one of his partners left for Israel, there was a larger and even more lucrative venture, a partnership in a major textile mill with a respected Pole. Legend has it that this audacious man escaped Poland in 1951 by flying his own bi-plane across the frontier. Eventually, he ended up in São Paolo where it was said his fortunes plummeted because he couldn't bear the fact that his wife had left him, and on top of that, for a Jew.

My father's mood in those first post-war years seems to have combined grimness with a high octane, almost manic energy. Perhaps it was also the mood of a Poland filled with rage and a simultaneous desire for reconstruction. Aron was like a car which couldn't stop revving, always on the move and in a major hurry, making up for the enforced passivity of the lost years of the war, hurrying out his hatred and his guilt. My mother says they never managed to finish a meal at the same time. She had hardly sat down when my father had already wolfed his food and got up from the table.

The narrative of life in those years has a frenzy to it as if time speeded up after the stupor of war. For my mother, there were frequent and extended holidays in country resorts or spa towns. Here she led the high life, dancing the night away at balls, entertaining courtiers under the vigilant eye of Staszek, who threw sand in their faces or aimed slingshots in an attempt to restitute family honour. When Aron came to spend a brief week or weekend and his son complained of his mother's behaviour, Aron carried on playing cards. Staszek was disgruntled. His father seemed more interested in an occasional flutter than in family honour. His son didn't understand. He didn't understand that Aron was consumed only by the desire to work, to earn and to escape Poland. But they couldn't leave. The principal reason that they couldn't leave was Sara. She refused to budge until Adek was returned to her. And Hania wouldn't go anywhere without her.

Early in '48, Sara has her first stroke. She is paralysed on the left side. It is her body's resistance to being moved. It is also the signal that she has begun to give up the hope that her son will be returned to her. This is all she has continued to live for.

She lies motionless in a high white bed, her white face and white hair lost amongst the white pillows. I can see her. See an unmoving ancient face framed by wisps of hair floating high, high above me on a tall metal-framed bed.

I think this image constitutes my first real memory. For a long time, I didn't know what it referred to. It was simply there – the bed so very high, the unmoving creased face floating in lofty whiteness, unattached to a body. The image terrified me. As children do, I must have picked up on the fraught emotions which attended my grandmother's hospitalisation. Only as an adult, when I was told of the manner of my grandmother's death, did image and narrative coalesce.

Judging by its atmosphere, one other memory I have seems to belong to the Poland of my childhood. No one else has been able to place it for me. In the memory I am sitting on a man's shoulders. He is very tall and certainly not my father. We are in the country. There are trees with white bark everywhere and as he carries me their leaves tickle my face. In front of us there are two high posts with a banner spread between them. We walk beneath it. We are in an enclave with a cluster of wooden cabins. The man takes me into one of these and puts me down. Then he pulls off his shoes. I stare at his feet and start to scream. He has no toes. His feet end in a round solid mass. I scream and scream.

For years and years this memory recurred, unplaceable, like a nightmare I had conjured up from childhood mists. Recently, I described it to my brother. The location meant something to him – some wooded campsite – but not the man. My partner suggested that there was a simple explanation: the stranger in the memory could well have lost his toes as a result of frostbite, hardly an uncommon experience in those who spent a portion of the war years living rough in the woods.

Death and war-wounds – my only childhood images of Poland.

In September '48, Staszek, now nine, was sent away to school in the mountain town of Bolkow near the Czech border. He says he was sent there because his mother wanted to get rid of him. Perhaps, her rumoured suitors apart, she simply had

enough to contend with between a small child and a paralysed
mother. Staszek was sent to Bolkow to attend a Jewish school.
It was time for him to interiorise his Jewishness. Near the
school there was a big Hagganah training camp. Staszek didn't
mind the training in frontier and military skills children were
given to prepare them for immigration to Israel, but he hated
the Yiddish classes he was forced to take. He refused to learn.
Later, in Canada, he repeated this refusal and was kicked out
of his Bar Mitzvah classes. The ambivalence towards Jewishness
runs deep in the family.

In October, Sara suffered a second stroke which paralysed
her right side. At 6.30 on the evening of the 13th, she died.
Depending on which documents one chooses to believe, she
was either sixty-two or sixty-eight years old. The only certainty
is that my mother had lost the last remaining member of her
family of origin. As if to contest this, she took on with
increased ardour the maternal certainty that Adek would still
be found.

Staszek was brought back from the failed experiment of
the Jewish school in Bolkow, only to be placed in a small
new Jewish school in Łódź. He hated this with equal passion. Luck of a kind or body speech contrived to shorten his
time there. Early in 1949, he was walking near one of the
many reconstruction sites when a plank scudded off a scaf-
folding and hit him on the head. Safely in bed for several
weeks, he developed appendicitis and had to be rushed to
hospital. Bedtime was prolonged. To speed his convales-
cence, my mother took him to stay with a friend in the
countryside. When they returned to Łódź, late in August,

Staszek committed the most dangerous act of his young life. He told the truth.

As a man of fifty-eight, he still doesn't know what led him to do it.

Throughout these post-war years, there had been many forbidding knocks on the door of the Legionov Street apartment. Not SS men, but Russian and latterly Polish secret service men. They came to conduct searches. They were looking for dollars or contraband or simply looking.

The well-rehearsed routine was that on their arrival, Hania politely and meticulously showed them round one corner of the apartment, while Staszek, the hoard soon tucked into his pockets or his coat, went off to play at a neighbour's.

This time, however, Hania was not home. She had taken me out for a walk. When the three policemen asked him whether his father's name was Zabłocki or Borensztejn, Staszek found himself replying, 'Both.'

The truth was treacherous.

He recognised that in the men's satisfied smiles. 'Tell your father we'll be back. Back in the morning.'

All Aron's Łódź business was conducted under the name Zabłocki. As events had proved, it was still safer not to be Jewish. The family's private documents – passports and visas – however, were under the name Borensztejn. And there were several of these now, wrapped in a white cloth in the drawer of the sideboard: visas for Cuba and Argentina and France, but not the long-awaited ones for the United States or Canada.

That evening, when Staszek told his parents of the secret

service men's visit, they realised they had to disappear. Hurriedly, they packed what they could and at five o'clock the following morning, they crammed into a droshki and boarded the first train to Warsaw. They spent two nights in a Warsaw hotel and from there moved to a small sanatorium town just outside the city. Through an intermediary, Aron arranged for at least a key-money transfer on the apartment in Łódź. But it was not money he was primarily worried about: there would be some thirty thousand dollars waiting for him in the New World, a tidy sum by his calculations. He had contacted his brother in New York again in the hope of a final response about American visas. He waited for a reply until the day after the Jewish New Year. Nothing came. The time for waiting, everyone then agreed, had run out.

We boarded the train for Paris. In her final act of heroism on Polish soil, Hania, in preparation for the inevitable search, managed to tuck all their dollars and valuables into a pipe between two carriages. Once across the border, she retrieved them.

I can see her breathing a sigh of relief and smiling. She is lucky, she thinks. She has always been lucky. And they are lucky. They will never return to Poland again.

Adek is certainly already in America.

PART THREE

Ghost Language

Ghost Language

My parents' war was over. But the war they had internalised didn't really end for a long time. It played out its pressures, its disguises and its pain in the living for at least the length of my childhood. And its traces lingered on. Like some ghost, it haunted our lives and appeared in odd places.

Writing this book has made some of these hauntings clearer to me. What often appeared as my parents' incomprehensible acts or perverse attitudes, a set of floating emotions which landed inappropriately on a given scene, are now grounded in the distorted world where they found their genesis. I can now understand how the fierce insecurities of war so permeated my parents' being, that they kept up the charade of two names and dual identities, long after they were particularly useful. I can understand why they sent me to convent schools, the mirrorings of Polish-Jewish life they enacted on Canadian soil. I can understand their heightened sensitivity to anti-Semitism, the discourse of racism which so marked them that they incorporated its ways of dividing up the world, even to their own detriment. In this last, of course, they were hardly alone.

Some of my own contradictions are also now clearer to me. The reactions of childhood, the rebellions of adolescence are after all in some measure perpetuations of the same family matter. In lesser or greater ways, they bear the stamp of repetition. From the vantage point of mid-life, I can now see why I would have wanted so quickly to shed a family name which had inevitably become imbued with shame and bore the mark of what in my parents' experience was a persecuted identity group. The residue of all this is that I still don't like fixed identities, bracketed or determined. I am wary of identity politics which, for all their good intentions, seem to me to bear a whiff of the Nazis' racist categories and are another way of closing one's eyes both to what we all share as humans and to complexities which can't be forced into single identities. More personally, I sometimes long for the freedom that writing pseudonymously gives one. Sometimes I secretly think that writing fiction, which is what I mostly do, is simply a way of acting out my mother's fabulations, while being able to insist on a certain honesty in everyday life.

Confronted now by my mother's pedestrian paranoia, her host of thieves and stolen objects, her suspicion of groups – even survivors' groups – I try to cool my anger and remind myself that there are deep and historic reasons for all this excess.

Since the second half of the sixties, which commentators characterise as the end of the period of wartime denial, much has been written in a psychoanalytic vein about Holocaust survivors and their children. Parenthetically, it is worth noting that the attention paid to survivors' psychic states grew hand in hand with legal interest. When the newly formed German Federal Republic, under the guidance of the Western Allies, instituted the Reparations or Wiedergutmachung legislation in 1953, lawyers were needed to press the cases of claimants damaged by the war. A whole new legal speciality emerged. At first, the rules for reparation were limited to physical claims. Amidst much anxiety and argument about the dishonour of taking blood money, both my parents made claims through a lawyer and received a pension: my father's was directly linked to ongoing back problems caused by his time in a forced labour camp.

Initially, there was no category in the Reparation laws for psychic damage caused by war. Trauma, at that time, was understood as a passing state: a wound which left no permanent scars. Persecution, the brutal inhumanity of the camps, being the subject of a master plan for extermination, were not understood as factors leading to psychiatric conditions. Yet survivors suffered from a host of psychosomatic ailments, as well as chronic depression, heightened anxiety and severe sleep disorders. In 1965, the rules governing Reparations were modified so as to allow some psychiatric conditions caused by war. But it was only with the lobbying of Vietnam veterans and their attorneys in the United States that trauma and post-traumatic stress syndrome with its wide range of symptoms made its way into the diagnostic manuals and earned its place as an 'illness' warranting claims – claims which can now include a wide variety of trauma-inducing circumstances and be laid at the charge of government or institution or family, with a price tag attached.

My parents had no discourse of traumatic illness available
to them and so they integrated their sufferings as best they
could into what they thought of as the experience of their
lives. Indeed, they would have been far too proud and too
intent on independence to consider that damage existed
which they weren't aware of. Any authority set up to 'know
better' was instantly suspect: they had already had far too
much of authority. It is perhaps because of their legacy that I
am perpetually in at least two minds about what is tanta-
mount to the 'medicalisation' of suffering and its effects.
Illness presupposes the possibility of cure and I'm not sure
that this is an appropriate register in which to consider the
magnitude of wartime experience. It was lived and then, if
survived, overlaid with other experience. People didn't recover
from it in the way one recovers from pneumonia given the
right dose of drugs.

Certainly my parents were deeply affected by their experience of the war – I hesitate to employ the word 'damaged' since
to use it presupposes that I know what undamaged beings are,
that I have a line on perfect psychic health. I don't. People are
too various. My parents were able to love and to work – which
is the maximum Freud sought for any of his patients. If they
did both in their own particular way, then that is what individuality is all about.

And yet . . .

With their own inflections, my parents shared with others
who lived through the Holocaust a range of problems which
the psy-professions have now described. States of panic, such
as my father's at border-crossings, are common and linked with

a fear of renewed persecution. So too are recurrent nightmares, combined with a terror of falling asleep. Social withdrawal, an inability to give words to the horror of lived wartime events, is prevalent. Like my mother, many suffer from free-floating anxiety. They also share a magical belief that lost ones will suddenly reappear.

I recognise bits of myself in other children of survivors, too. There is sometimes a parent-child dynamic at work in which a messianic hope is attached to the child who must enact great deeds to justify prior loss. This can be felt by the young as a burden or as an electric charge, an act of faith. Children can experience the tragic weight of their parents' past lives as something which is so much greater than their ordinary, everyday plaints, that these can never be voiced or shared. As a result, their own feelings are nullified. Alternately, this burden from the past can be experienced as something children need to compete with to gain parental attention or favour, so that they find themselves undertaking ever more dangerous risks or enacting bruising dramas. The degradation parents suffered, the blanket guilt they carry at having survived the dead, can also turn children into suspicious persecutors: if they survived or escaped, was it the result of treachery, some perfidious act at another's expense? Do their parents, in some mysterious way, deserve to be punished?

In the ghost language which passes between the generations, all this played itself out over time between my parents, my brother and myself. On top of it, beside it, around it, there was the language of everyday practicalities and getting on with life. I still do not think we were particularly unhappy children.

We live at a time when it seems all childhoods are retrospectively so fraught and miserable that the adults who contain them can pin blame and sometimes go to court in search of compensation. But life is in some measure also the story we tell ourselves about it. Stories are complicated, textured things. They contain ups and downs. Happiness, for me, is not a bland, placid and seamless stretch, but complexity, a rich fabric of many shades, a tapestry which can include anger and internal battles and wonder. And yes, even periods of unhappiness.

I suspect that the visible differences between my parents, in the way they interiorised the war, and in their spoken attitudes and gestural asides, permitted my brother and me to work and think through some of the implications of this wartime residue. Where my mother insisted on forgetting the worst and forgiving, my father's internal rage kept the worst alive and expressed itself in fierce condemnation of all things German and Polish. Though as a child I hated their battles, the differences between them forced us to think. The Holocaust presented to us was not a distant, unitary horror, an inviolable absolute, like some secular religion through which a collective identity built on suffering is consolidated. They had lived through it and their memories particularised it for us. Within the frame of a hideous and demented racist regime which perpetrated unique atrocities, there were good people and bad people. The possibility of human agency, of individuals acting, was kept alive. That helps.

The rest of this story is not without its ironies.

On our last day in Warsaw, Monica and I are strolling

towards the Old Town when we see a crowd gathered in front of the Presidential Palace. There are ranked soldiers standing to attention. A limousine pulls up and disgorges three men. The band begins to play. Strains of 'Hatikvah', the Israeli national anthem, fill the air. When Monica asks a policeman what is going on, he doesn't answer. Instead he rebukes us for crossing the street. Jaywalking is prohibited. I speak loudly in English and he has the belated courtesy to recognise us as tourists and tell us he doesn't know what is happening. In our reasonable way, we assume that Israeli dignitaries are visiting the President.

Later, in front of the Tomb of the Unknown Soldier, I come upon a second ceremonial. Again the soldiers are ranked, a limousine pulls up and two men get out. One is African, the second presumably his host. Once more, the band plays 'Hatikvah'. The dignitaries stand to attention, then parade down the aisle formed by the soldiers and lay a wreath at the Tomb. I wait for the ceremony to end before asking one of the soldiers who the visiting dignitary was. An ambassador from Oman, he tells me. 'Oman?' I echo. 'But the band was playing the Israeli anthem?' He gives me a blank look and shrugs.

As we drive to the airport, I relate these curious scenes to Andrzej Latko. I cannot understand why 'Hatikvah' should be played to an Omani or African ambassador. Andrzej's eyes twinkle more merrily than ever. He chuckles. 'It's very simple. Obviously our military band learned the Israeli anthem so well, they now play it for everyone.'

Polish-Israeli diplomatic relations, resumed only in 1990 after a twenty-two-year lapse, are evidently on an upswing.

*

When I return home to London, there is a message for me
from the Tracing Service of the International Red Cross. I have
an odd sense that the gods of research are mocking me. I have
travelled some 2,000 kilometres to Poland in the hope of a
trace of Adek and all the time it may have been waiting for me
back in London. None the less, I am filled with excitement. I
ring the Red Cross early the next morning. The woman in
charge is on the case: she gives me two more numbers to contact. I do so instantly. At the Polish Section of the Ministry of
Defence which holds files on Polish forces under British
wartime command, they have a computerised data base. They
run a search while I wait. Two Adolf Lipszycs turn up. My
heart pounds. I didn't realise I cared so much.

But when the details emerge, neither the places nor dates of
birth of these two Lipszycs remotely tally with those of my
mother's brother. Sadness overtakes me. I would have liked to
have known how my uncle died. It would permit an appropriate mourning. It would put a few of the ghosts to rest. If he
had appeared in the Ministry of Defence archives, we would
know he had died in battle or even as a prisoner of war. We
would know when and how.

As it is, the fantasies are rampant. During the war, there
seemed to be more ways of dying than of living. The last trace
we have of Adek is in Warsaw in the summer of 1943. We do
not know whether, as seems likely, he was a fighter in the Polish
Resistance forces. If so, was he shot in one of the many Nazi
acts of reprisal? Was he rounded up in the street, only to be sent
to a labour camp or worse, discovered as a Jew and transported
to a death camp? Did he die during one of the blood-stained

days of the Warsaw Uprising, trapped in a sewer or under the rubble of falling buildings or in a dense wood illuminated only by shell fire? Does he lie in one of the many mass graves of unnamed dead? Could he have been one of the seven thousand tragic victims of the *Thielbek* and *Cap Arcona* catastrophe of May 3, 1945, when two Baltic sea-liners – carrying thousands of prisoners hastily evacuated from Auschwitz and North German concentration camps before the Allies could discover them – were accidentally strafed by the RAF? For months, well after the war's end, unidentifiable bodies clad in striped pyjamas were washed on to the shores of Lübeck Bay.

Death is endlessly, horribly inventive.

One story I encountered during my research into Adek's life and disappearance illuminates how fantasy works when facts are scarce. It was told to me only on my repeated insistence and in hesitant whispers by a friend of my parents, who attributed it to another acquaintance, now in a home in Israel. In this story, Adek worked for 'them'.

'Who?' I ask, ever naïve.

'Them. The Gestapo.' The friend looks over his shoulder as if 'they' might still be listening – even now in this apartment in the centre of Paris. 'I don't believe it, of course.' But he believes it enough to repeat it.

I weigh up the known and the unknown. I imagine Adek in the way he has always been portrayed to me – a young, fiery rebel against *shtetl* ways, proud enough of his Jewishness to link himself to the Zionist cause, yet never passive or enduring, a risk-taker, a fighter. The story of Gestapo affiliation doesn't really tally. Adek saved too many Jewish lives. I can only conclude that the

masquerade which allowed him to fraternise with Germans was
obviously so good that even the small-town Jews were taken in.
But I don't know for certain. In this version of his disappearance,
he might still be living the high life of an octogenarian somewhere in Uruguay.

I don't tell my mother this story. In any case, on my return
from Poland, she doesn't really want to hear. The treasured documents from the Jewish Historical Institute, her mother's death
certificate, nothing captures her interest. Even the photographs
of the towns of her pre-war youth receive only a cursory glance.
She pauses once or twice, when pressed, or remarks that
Andrzej Latko looks very old. It is too late. All she really takes
in is that I have been away for far too long and now I am back
I am to be punished for my absence.

The punishment is insidious. It takes the form of telling me
and my children and anyone who will listen how wonderful I
once was – no longer, of course. I was a good girl who never
minded being left alone; a brilliant pupil, so that she never had
to go to any school meetings, like the ones I'm constantly running off to. I was the first woman in Québec to drive at the age
of sixteen. I had hundreds of marriage proposals from rich men
who proffered diamonds. Fact and fantasy blur in an orgy of
repetition. The only thing that is certain is that after I left
Canada – a few blips aside when our lives happened once more
to coincide – it was downhill all the way. Her negativity
enshrouds my children as well, as if they, too, despite their
youth, already had all their best moments behind them – ones
they shared more actively with her. I have to remind them and

myself, that this is the reduced voice of old age speaking, not their grandmother.

During the time that I write about her war, something she has encouraged me to do for years, she all but refuses to speak about it. Certainly it ceases to be one of her preoccupations. I don't know whether this is because she feels I have stolen it from her or that she has given it to me. In any case, the onus has been transferred. As she approaches her own end, I have taken over her dead. She only mentions the war now, when she needs to insist that her cloudy intelligence or acuity far exceed mine.

'If you had lived through a war, like I have ...'

I'm glad I haven't.

I try to help her in her lonely and often demented fragility by finding a carer to live with her, by arranging visits from social services or volunteers. She locks them all out of the house or pretends not to hear the doorbell, though she hears it well enough when I press it. 'My mother lived with me through the worst of times,' she moans. 'The world has changed horribly. It's a dreadful place.'

'Yes,' I acquiesce and stifle guilt, best as I can. I am not prepared to give up partner and children and work to immure myself with her endless plaints and what I feel is a contagious discourse of madness.

Her stubborn wilfullness, I tell myself, is all that remains of her old self. She is still indomitable – even if not always for her own good.

One other aspect of her character seems to have remained intact. I see it in operation each time I take her on one of her

regular visits to the doctor. All her aches and pains, her
repeated phone calls to the clinic and cries for help, disappear
as soon as she sees him. She never presents a list of ailments:
instead she sits on the edge of her chair, looks up at him
coquettishly and smiles. Her eyelashes fluttering, she tells him
what a wonderful man he is and engages on one of her rambling narratives about the past. She flirts. She charms. For a
brief span nothing but that matters.

Her seductiveness still has the power to trouble and embarrass me, just as it did in childhood when stories of her
innumerable conquests were oft repeated, sometimes when
actual admirers were present.

A scene comes back to me. There are guests in the house
and we are all sitting in the newly decorated living room with
its L-shaped sofa re-covered in some brocade imitation of
French Provençal. I must be about fourteen and I am morti-
fied by my mother's light little preening laugh as she says to
the assembled company, 'He was so in love with me, that
Russian. There was nothing we could do about it. Nothing.'
She glances at my father for confirmation. He doesn't seem to
be listening. He puffs at his cigarette. I race from the room. I
am filled with that puritanical revulsion so prevalent in
teenagers. How can she speak like that! In front of everyone.
In front of her husband.

It was not that I didn't consider my mother beautiful – quite
the contrary. But in my eyes she was far too old for sexuality,
let alone infidelity. Her youth was unimaginable. In any case,
such things were not to be talked about out loud. And the
more she talked, the more I consoled myself that she retailed

such stories to build up her own self-image. These scores of past admirers were just balloon talk.

Later, when I knew what affairs were, I speculated again about my mother's rumoured ones, which she in conventional fashion had always denied: she would shake her head dismissively and call my brother silly, a fantasist, if he brought up the matter of the KGB colonel and my doubtful paternity. I decided to believe her, rather than my brother. After all, she was so visibly attached to and dependent on my father. And it seemed to me she was far too prim about sex and the body ever to have done much more than flirt. She was distinctly not a post-'68 woman. It was power she was interested in, not sex, I decided.

But perhaps I needed to think that then. And I now realise – given that power and sex are not necessarily distinguishable – that I could easily have been wrong. There is my father's final delirium, in which he imagined my mother whoring with the Gestapo officer-doctors, to take into account, aside from my brother's contentions. Though in an altogether different spirit from both of the jealous males in the family, I too, at times, have relished the notion of a wildly adventurous mother, going to any lengths to secure her aims. Wartime, after all, always loosens sexual morality. And right up until the moment I left home, there were all those devoted suitors ...

Whatever the reality of her love life, it is no longer verifiable. And in a way now, the mystery that parental sexuality always remains no matter what proofs exist seems to me preferable. What is clear to me at long last and after many years of ambivalence is that my mother's flirtation has a sweetness about it. An innocence, too. It speaks of her own kindness and generosity: she would like to seduce the world into returning good to her.

Now, when she can't, paranoia steps into its place. There is no way of reasoning her out of it. One delusion that takes hold of her and refuses to shift has to do with her neighbour climbing down her non-existent chimney. He steals precious objects from her locked bedroom, to which he has also stolen the keys. He may do far worse. She has called the police in several times, communicated with other neighbours. Neither my rage nor proof, nor calm persuasion can shake her belief.

One night, when she repeats all this to me her conviction is such that I find myself afraid as I again unlock the door she is so certain will open on the interloper. I hesitate, fumble with missing keys I have somehow found. There is no one there. Of course. I knew that. It is her panic which has overtaken me. My brave mother is more frightened than she has ever been. Frightened of a Jewish neighbour. The physical fact of that fear, after all these months of immersing myself in her courageous, younger self, brings with it a great sadness.

The sadness demands that I contain my irritation and often my rage at some of her foibles, such as her oft-reiterated opening gambit of 'You know me; I never complain' – before launching into a torrent of plaints. It comes to me that her idea of herself is fixed in a prior body: it has never changed, despite changing realities. Somewhere buried inside her, like lost civilisations, are other selves who never complain, who are shrewd about the world, who are rivetingly attractive and yes, never afraid. They use her lips to speak. Maybe that's what old age is about. If it is, it frightens me far more than death. I realise that it is also for that fearful, tattering bit of me that I have needed to reinvent my mother's earlier selves.

A dream from Poland pursues me the length of my first week at home. In it I am lying supine, whether on the ground or on a bed isn't clear. All around me the people are very tall. There are many of them and their voices are loud. They talk and talk. They speak in a babble I can't understand but all its intonations and rhythms mark it out as Polish. I can't speak. My tongue won't move properly. And I need to get away from this clamour of sound. I must. The noise is unbearable. But nothing my mouth does produces the requisite speech which I know will lift me above the babble. I raise my head. There is a barrier above it. Thick, solid wood. I can't break through it. Only if I break through will the clamour subside. I press and push. And push and wake.

Everything tells me that this dream belongs to infancy, to that liminal moment when babble is about to merge into language. My journey to Poland, the continual sounds of the language, have thrust me back to a time when I was learning to speak. Speak Polish. The difficulty of speech, the overwhelming density of language is the barrier the child in the dream can't quite break through. But nor can the adult who I am. I thought the trip to Poland would help activate the language inside me. It didn't. The barrier is still there. In Polish I am as mute as an infant.

Perhaps one can't speak to ghosts, only listen.

My first letter from Poland is not from a ghost. Nor is it in Polish. My young Łódź attorney, in another course in this feast of ironies, has chosen to write to me in German. So the letter which tells me that no further trace of Adek Lipszyc has been found comes in a language he might have preferred not to hear again. The letter also informs me that no record of the birth of Elzbieta Borensztejn (or Borensztajn) – that is, me – exists in the Łódź Registry archive. In an apologetic tone, Herr or Pan Kubiak writes that often Jews didn't bother to register their children or registered them all at once. Would I like to suggest some alternative birth dates?

Would I ever! But I don't. Losing one's birth is rather easier than losing one's dead.

A month later, a second letter arrives, again in German, bearing more of what Pan Kubiak calls bad news. This time he has been to the Łódź Registry of Residents. And this time no one in my family seems to exist. The slate is clean. Official history refuses to coincide with family memory. Everything is open to invention.

At Christmas my brother comes to London from Montréal. He has not been here for some five years. After a week of mulling over the past, we both decide we would like to visit our father's grave. Our mother doesn't want to come. Throughout the period of her son's longed-for visit, she all but refuses to leave her house as if she is afraid it may not be there on her return. Her sense that the world is filled with predators increases with the fragility of her body. It is perhaps that very body she most fears will not be there to await her on her return.

We drive along the Great North Road and turn off just before the M25 in order to pass over it. It is a cold, blustery day.

As the cemetery appears in the distance, my brother exclaims, 'It's snowing!' But what he sees is the whiteness of ranked tombstones against a steel-grey sky.

We walk quickly through the flat expanse towards our father's grave. I don't know why, but when we reach it, I start to cry. I have never wept here before. I hide my tears in the sudden lash of driving rain. It comes in great bursts of water and then disappears to let through a glimmer of wintry light. In the distance there is a constant rumble of sound, not thunder though, but the noise of the traffic on the motorway.

I wonder how my father feels about being buried so close to this speeding cavalcade. And then I remember how, when we first arrived in Canada and he took driving lessons, the instructor had to learn some Polish to be able to shout at him, 'Pomalu! Pomalu! Slowly! Slowly!' because he was going far too fast.

For a man who was always running, perhaps he has come to rest in the right place – and in the very country which produced the textiles which helped him endure the war.

I think my brother and I are both happy that with all the lost dead, our father at least, is in a place where we can find him.

AFTERWORD

In the years since I wrote this memoir, my mother has joined my father in that blustery cemetery in North London. She died on 21 January, 2002. Her mind had left her some two years before her life. Its deep recesses of history had given way to frightening hallucinations and then to a great and general forgetting.

Latterly when I would go and visit her in the nursing home where she spent her last years, she would look up at me with her clear blue eyes and say, 'I think we've met before. Yes, I think we may have met before.'

She had no idea that I had seen her a day or a week ago, not to mention been her daughter for a rather considerable time. Her words, often spoken in Yiddish or Polish, were an iteration of politeness: perhaps forms and structures of language really do occupy a deeper part of the brain than individual memory. Yet, the warmth with which she grasped my hands, her unwillingness to let go, allowed me to think that other more bodily familiarities persisted. This may well have been more wish than fact. However tense relations with our parents are at occasional points in our lives, we like to suppose they have *known* us.

For her grandchildren, whom she had once been devoted to, the eerie lack of recognition was even more daunting. I would remind them of the strangeness of Alzheimer's, the forgetting disease, and that the person in front of them was and wasn't their grandmother. Now that she had all the necessary identity papers that had so preoccupied her during the war years, it seemed she didn't really have herself.

The diagnosis had arrived some three years before she ceased to recognise us and to mark any passage of time. The naming of her condition as neurological rather than psychological in origin at first felt like a boon. It absolved us of any guilt for her occasional mad states: our sometime lack of attentiveness wasn't responsible for her decline.

And yet, and yet . . .

The trouble with clinical descriptions is that they tell you little about how the individual will inflect the particular condition – what will be forgotten and what remembered, which areas of judgement will be impaired, which aspects of personality will come to the forefront and which vanish. Nor, of course, do they signal when the person is acting 'in character' and where 'the disease' has taken over. There is no easy clinical guide for coping with the irrational behaviour of near ones or what it will trigger in us.

Having long been interested in the psychology and politics of memory, my mother's forgetting sent me off to the brain scientists in search of answers. But whatever I learned couldn't stop her dying. And when she did, it was technically of a cold.

She had caught it after Christmas. The nursing home rang late one night to tell me it was affecting her breathing. When I came to see her the next morning, she was so small and still and motionless on her bed that I thought she might have gone without anyone noticing. She looked like a girl, her face unlined and somehow utterly at peace. The sides of her lips were turned up in what might have been a smile or simply the shape of features I had never seen in complete repose. When I emerged from her room, the doctor asked whether I wanted her taken to hospital. In thrall to that sense of peace about her and what I imagined would be her distress at waking amid the noise and garish lights of a ward, I said no.

The next day she was dead.

I want to say we missed her. But in fact we were relieved. She had been gone for so long; nor had the burden of her been easy. When I started to dream about her, at first the dreams were terrible. She appeared in a netted chicken coop, making angry sounds, at once a giant pecking creature and a raging old woman behind barbed wire, a kind of Baba Yaga of folklore. She was angry at me for having 'locked her up' – in her nursing home, I thought, and she scared me.

Gradually as the years passed and I grew older and a little frailer, I began to understand her last years better. There's a kind of panic that sets in for women when attractiveness can no longer be counted on to induce the kindness of strangers. I began to grow friendlier towards her fragilities and fears, which I hadn't wanted to relax into before since she was, after all, my mother and the tipping of the power balance has to be negotiated at every stage. She began to appear in my dreams in a more beneficent guise. She was often young, innocent, cavorting: she would guide or frolic and slip effortlessly into my daughter or me.

These familial slippages are ever interesting. I realised in photographs that having always thought I looked like my father, I in fact looked like her, colouring apart. So did my son. It was he, who suddenly manifested an interest in his grandmother and set out to make a film about her. He trawled through nursing homes, including the one she had been in. He talked to staff and to residents. He read what I had written about her and made a powerful short film, *Ex Memoria*. The film beautifully and moodily marries Sara Kestelman and Natalie Press. The first plays a disoriented old woman immersed in her own mind, pushed hither and thither in a wheelchair by attendants who know nothing more about her than the decaying body she inhabits. The second plays her when young – a fetching woman in some patently Eastern European wood where something terrible happens. 'Some memories fade. Others keep returning' the tagline on the DVD reads.

Memory is a subject that doesn't leave this family alone. Perhaps it's no coincidence that my daughter studied history.

As for me, the whole matter of my parents and Central Europe continued to haunt me and turned into a later novel *The Memory Man*. Maybe it was simply the number of letters I received about *Losing the Dead*: the book seemed to have touched so many people and many wrote to me telling me their own stories as well.

Before writing these paragraphs for the new edition, I reread the memoir: one's own life put out in the public sphere becomes someone else's, so I might as well have been reading a stranger's story. I was pleased to find, however, that at this distance my mother had turned into a remarkable heroine, and my father into a character with more dimensions than I remembered. Their story was full of intrigue, pain, the horror of war and racism, the ordeal and hope of migration, and meanings I hadn't altogether grasped while writing it. It became even clearer to me that in my family while I was growing up, there were no lost paradises and no nostalgia, not until more than half a century separated my mother from some of the key events in her life. Until dotage, my parents lived lives focused on what could be built for the future. Losing their dead was a necessary part of that trajectory. Perhaps my little volume is a coin cast into a fountain, a wish that I won't lose mine, and that returns, at least in prose, are possible.

The book is, of course, about the various kinds of memory and forgetting that shape our lives as well as our collectivities – our national, ethnic or religious groups. Since I wrote it, memory studies – theoretical, fictional, autobiographical and psychological – have all burgeoned. That's probably as it should be in a period where so many of our memories have been displaced into clouds, computers and social networking sites. Humans ever worry about and study disappearing phenomena. I guess this is my contribution to the field.

Despite the many changes for the better that have taken place in Poland since I went there to do my research – including the opening of the Museum of the History of Polish Jews on the site of the former Warsaw Ghetto – I was glad to find that what I had written stood the test of over a decade. I hope others may too. Remembering – as the poets and writers have long known and neuroscientists have now concurred – is also a form of imagining: giving life to my parents' war and its rumbling aftermath was one of the most intimately engrossing tasks I have ever taken on as a writer.

Lisa Appignanesi
July 2013

ACKNOWLEDGEMENTS

Very special thanks are due to my brother,
Stanley Borenstein, who gave me the benefit of his
time and knowledge, as well as to my parents' friends,
Jonas and Bella Sebrien and Andrzej Latko, now sadly
deceased. Monica Holmes was a constant support, Jenny
Uglow the finest of editors and Lennie Goodings the best
of publishers. My thanks, too, to Victor Ross and
Victoria Pepe who helped prepare this edition.

MAD, BAD AND SAD
A HISTORY OF WOMEN AND THE MIND
DOCTORS FROM 1800 TO THE PRESENT

Endlessly fascinating'
Independent on Sunday

Mad, bad and sad. From the depression suffered by Virginia Woolf
and Sylvia Plath to the mental anguish and addictions of iconic beauties
Zelda Fitzgerald and Marilyn Monroe. From Freud and Jung and the
radical breakthroughs of psychoanalysis to Lacan's construction of
a modern movement and the new women-centred therapies – this is
the story of how we have understood mental disorders and extreme
states of mind in women over the last two hundred years and how
we conceive of them today, when more and more of our inner life
and emotions have become a matter for medics and therapists.

'Subtle, textured and enthralling'
Sunday Times

'A glittering intellectual history of women,
madness and the mind doctors'
Melanie McGrath, *Sunday Telegraph*

'Fascinating . . . In this sweeping, humane and formidably researched
study Appignanesi does what all the very best investigative writers
and journalists do: she raises questions for us to answer'
Carmen Callil, *Daily Telegraph*

'*Mad, Bad and Sad* is constantly interesting . . .
wonderfully engaging and enlightening'
Rachel Bowlby, *Independent*

'The triumph of *Mad, Bad and Sad* is to mix evocative case studies with
potted histories of the great and good of psychology and psychiatry . . .
an intelligent and academically rigorous study'
Observer

ALL ABOUT LOVE
ANATOMY OF AN UNRULY EMOTION

'I LOVE *All About Love*'
Hanif Kureishi

Unruly, unpredictable, love is a maddening deity. In this
insightful and eloquent meditation on that many-splendoured thing,
Lisa Appignanesi draws on history, philosophy, literature, popular
culture and her own experience in order to tangle with
the psychology of love through the span of our lives.

'Appignanesi carries her knowledge lightly, dipping into Derrida
one minute and *Mad Men* the next. The book is full
of historical curiosities and morsels of gossip'
Jemima Lewis, *Mail on Sunday*

'A useful guide to passion'
Iain Finlayson, *The Times*

'Thoughtful and fascinating . . . With a sensitive eye she charts
changing attitudes . . . Measured and wise'
Rosemary Goring, *Herald*

virago

To buy any of our books and to find out more about Virago Press and Virago Modern Classics, our authors and titles, as well as events and book club forum, visit our websites

www.virago.co.uk
www.littlebrown.co.uk

and follow us on Twitter

@ViragoBooks

To order any Virago titles p & p free in the UK, please contact our mail order supplier on:

+ 44 (0)1832 737525

Customers not based in the UK should contact the same number for appropriate postage and packing costs.